A Dozen
Diamonds
From
Daniel

A Dozen
Diamonds
From
Daniel

Dr. Raymond Barber

SWORD of the LORD
PUBLISHERS
P. O. BOX 1099, MURFREESBORO, TN 37133

Printed and Bound in the United States of America

Table of Contents

Foreword

Introduction

Foreword

The messages in this book were preached in a series of messages in 1991 from the pulpit of Worth Baptist Church in Fort Worth, Texas.

Prophecy is a favorite subject of mine, inasmuch as I have taught courses on the Major-Minor Prophets in Bible colleges for almost thirty-five years.

No Old Testament prophet gives us a clearer understanding of God's unfolding plan for the ages than Daniel, who is called "the beloved prophet of God." In fact, only Daniel gives us a panorama of the "Times of the Gentiles," which extends from the destruction of Jerusalem by Nebuchadnezzar and the Babylonians in 586 B.C. until the revelation of Christ to establish His kingdom upon the earth to reign for a thousand years.

Daniel interprets Nebuchadnezzar's dream in chapter two as symbolizing the four great world empires, the remnants of which make up the ecclesiastical-political Babylon, which is to be destroyed by the brightness of our Lord's revelation.

The prayer of my heart is that God will use these messages to enlighten the reader in the development of eschatological events as prophesied by Daniel.

Introduction

Daniel is commonly referred to as one of the Major Prophets. It is not given this standing because of the size of the book but because of its stature.

It not only contains the marvelous accounts of Daniel in the lions' den and the three Hebrew children in the fiery furnace but also some of the most dramatic foretelling of events God ever gave.

The man Daniel was a major prophet in every sense of the word. His clean life, his powerful preaching, his wisdom, his strong stand for right and condemnation of sin, his prayer life, together with the precise revelations of the future God gave to him and through him, make him stand out above his peers.

The prophecy of the fall of Babylon was unbelievable but was fulfilled almost immediately. The detailed descriptions of the image, the beasts, the seventy weeks and other things to come stand tall among all prophetic utterances.

Many have been fulfilled, and that gives us a solid basis to believe those remaining will yet be fulfilled.

Dr. Raymond Barber takes the years of study and preparation he has invested to teach this great book in the college classroom as well as in his church and brings the cream of his work to us in this volume.

As the publishers, we pray this book will be a blessing, used to help us better understand our Lord and His Word, and will cause us to look with greater anticipation for "that blessed hope, and the glorious appearing of the great God and our Saviour Jesus Christ."

—Sword of the Lord Publishers

─── *Outline* 1:1–21 ───────────

The Smartest Man in Babylon

Introduction

Story of Daniel's captivity: 606 B.C.

First of three deportations to Babylon:

1. 606 B.C.
2. 597 B.C.
3. 586 B.C.—Destruction of Jerusalem

NOTE: Jerusalem was the "City of God."
- It contained the temple of God.
- It produced the Word of God.
- It housed the prophets of God.

NOTE: Tragically enough, the people of God...
...desecrated the temple of God.
...despised the Word of God.
...destroyed the prophets of God.

NOTE: Because of these sins they suffered the wrath of God.

NOTE: Only prophet to give panoramic view of history of the world from days of Nebuchadnezzar to kingdom of Christ.

NOTE: Daniel is called among prophets:
1. Chronologer
2. Historian
3. Politician

NOTE: Name means "God Is My Judge"
Date of ministry: 606–533 B.C.

Message

I. SOURCE OF DANIEL'S WISDOM

> **NOTE:** "God gave..." (vs. 17)
> "If any of you..." (James 1:5–8)
> Prov. 9:8–10
>
> **NOTE:** Daniel's Teacher: God (Isa. 48:17, 18)
> Daniel's text: Word of God (Ps. 119:11)
> Daniel's tuition: resources of God—paid!

II. SCOPE OF DANIEL'S WISDOM

- School: Three years (vs. 5)
- Studied
- Final exam: "...*stood they before the king*" (vs. 19).
- Graduation diploma: written and signed by Nebuchadnezzar

> **NOTE:** Verse 20

III. SHOWING OF DANIEL'S WISDOM

QUESTION: "How did Daniel show just how smart he was?"

ANSWER: I suggest three ways:

1. Physical appearance (vss. 3, 4)
   - A healthy body is a great asset in life.
   - Temple of the Spirit of God (I Cor. 6:19, 20)
   - A Christian should look like a Christian.
2. Spiritual dedication (vs. 8)
   a. Strange place—Babylon
      - A myrtle tree is a myrtle tree, even in the desert.
      - Geography should not change behavior.
      - Young men, don't be blinded by the bright lights of Babylon.

b. Strange people—pagans
c. Strange procedure—brainwashing (vs. 7)

> **NOTE:** Daniel could handle lions at age ninety
> because he learned to handle temptation
> at age nineteen.

3. Emotional stability (vss. 11–13)

> **NOTE:** In the midst of a pagan society, Daniel
> showed restraint.

- Character—firm;
- Conviction—forceful;
- Courage—fearless;
- Courtesy—fraternal.

Conclusion

A summary of Daniel's "college days": Babylon.

CHAPTER ONE

 The Smartest Man in Babylon

I shall read all twenty-one verses of Daniel, chapter 1.

1. *In the third year of the reign of Jehoiakim king of Judah came Nebuchadnezzar king of Babylon unto Jerusalem, and besieged it.*

2. *And the Lord gave Jehoiakim king of Judah into his hand, with part of the vessels of the house of God: which he carried into the land of Shinar* [that is, to the land of Babylon] *to the house of his god; and he brought the vessels into the treasure house of his god.*

3. *And the king spake unto Ashpenaz the master of his eunuchs, that he should bring certain of the children of Israel, and of the king's seed, and of the princes;*

4. *Children in whom was no blemish, but well favoured, and skillful in all wisdom, and cunning in knowledge, and understanding science, and such as had ability in them to stand in the king's palace, and whom they might teach the learning and the tongue of the Chaldeans* [or the Babylonians].

5. *And the king appointed them a daily provision of the king's meat, and of the wine which he drank: so nourishing them three years, that at the end thereof they might stand before the king.*

6. *Now among these were of the children of Judah, Daniel, Hananiah, Mishael, and Azariah:*

7. *Unto whom the prince of the eunuchs gave names: for he gave unto Daniel the name of Belteshazzar; and to Hananiah, of Shadrach; and to Mishael, of Meshach; and to Azariah, of Abed-nego.*

8. *But Daniel purposed in his heart that he would not defile himself with the portion of the king's meat, nor with the wine which he drank: therefore he requested of the prince of the eunuchs that he might not defile himself.*

9. *Now God had brought Daniel into favour and tender love with the prince of the eunuchs.*

10. *And the prince of the eunuchs said unto Daniel, I fear my lord the king, who hath appointed your meat and your drink: for why should he see your faces worse liking than the children which are of your sort? then shall ye make me endanger my head to the king.*

11. *Then said Daniel to Melzar, whom the prince of the eunuchs had set over Daniel, Hananiah, Mishael, and Azariah,*

12. *Prove thy servants, I beseech thee, ten days; and let them give us pulse to eat, and water to drink.*

13. *Then let our countenances be looked upon before thee, and the countenance of the children that eat of the portion of the king's meat: and as thou seest, deal with thy servants.*

14. *So he consented to them in this matter, and proved them ten days.*

15. *And at the end of ten days their countenances appeared fairer and fatter in flesh than all the children which did eat the portion of the king's meat.*

16. *Thus Melzar took away the portion of their meat, and the wine that they should drink; and gave them pulse* [that is, beans or some kind of hyssop upon which beans grow].

17. *As for these four children, God gave them knowledge and*

skill in all learning and wisdom: and Daniel had understanding in all visions and dreams.

18. *Now at the end of the days that the king had said he should bring them in, then the prince of the eunuchs brought them in before Nebuchadnezzar.*

19. *And the king communed with them; and among them was found none like Daniel, Hananiah, Mishael, and Azariah: therefore stood they before the king.*

20. *And in all matters of wisdom and understanding, that the king enquired of them, he found them ten times better than all the magicians and astrologers that were in all his realm.*

21. *And Daniel continued even unto the first year of king Cyrus.*

What a remarkable story! God is a wonderful writer, wouldn't you say? The Holy Spirit gave to Daniel, the author of this book, these words. The story of Daniel is the story of captivity. No period in all the history of the Jews was more distressing and disturbing than these days in which he lived.

These attacks were made against Jerusalem by King Nebuchadnezzar and the armies of Babylon. The first came in 606 B.C.; the second, in 597 B.C.; and the third, in 586 B.C.

In 606 B.C. (in the third year of Jehoiakim, at the besieging of the city of Jerusalem and its attack by Nebuchadnezzar), Daniel was taken captive into Babylon. When the second attack came in 597 B.C., Ezekiel, who becomes an outstanding prophet, is taken into captivity. In the year 586 B.C., the most devastating of all the attacks, the Temple at Jerusalem was destroyed, the walls of the city torn down, the people taken into captivity, with only a residue remaining.

That marked the beginning of a period in history known as the "Times of the Gentiles."

The destruction of Jerusalem in 586 B.C. brought havoc to the nation Israel and the kingdom of Judah. Jerusalem was the city of God. It first enters the biblical record in Genesis 15, where the writer talks about the king of Salem, Salem being Jerusalem. Jerusalem means "fountain of peace." Ironically, Jerusalem has probably enjoyed fewer years of peace than any major city in all the world. No less than forty-six times she has been sacked and burned by enemy armies, none more devastating than 586 B.C. Remember, the city of God, Jerusalem, contained the Temple of God, built by Solomon over a period of seven years and at the cost in our currency today of multiplied billions of dollars.

Not only did Jerusalem house the Temple of God, but it produced the Word of God. The living Word of God came out of Jerusalem for the most part. God raised up His men and put the Word in their hearts, and the Bible says that "all scripture is given by inspiration of God." The Bible says that holy men of God spake, as they were carried along, or moved, by the Holy Spirit.

The city of Jerusalem is the city of the Bible. Not only that: Jerusalem housed the prophets of God. Tragically enough, the people of God *desecrated* the Temple of God, *despised* the Word of God and *destroyed* the prophets of God. And because of their sins against God, they suffered the wrath of God.

America is following the same pattern. What happened in Jerusalem? Homosexuality, sexual promiscuity, idol worship, apathy and indifference. In fact, the prophet goes through and laments: 'If I can just find a man anywhere in the city who is on fire for God, who believes in God; if I can just find some warmhearted somebody who is concerned, who has compassion, someone who cares.'

We have almost come to that in our day. Preachers are going up and down America asking, "Where are the people who care for souls? Where are those who care for the Gospel? Where are the people who care for God, for Christ, for the Bible, for the church?"

In forty years of ministry, I have never seen a time when more people were as apathetic as now. Fewer, it seems, are genuinely concerned. I don't mean just have the attitude, "Well, I hope the church will prosper"—naturally, everybody would say that; but I'm talking about those willing to pay the price. I'm talking about sacrificial giving and living. I'm talking about sacrificial going after sinners. I'm talking about reading the Bible, about enjoying the Word of God and revival from God.

Where are such people who really want revival? I ask you a rhetorical question: How many of you really want revival this summer? What price are you willing to pay for revival? It will not happen with our coming together for an hour on Sunday morning or an hour on Sunday night. Revival will come out of the closet, with us on our knees. And revivals do not come with people being saved. They get Christians ready to go out and win souls and bring the lost in to be saved.

Psalm 9:17 says, "The wicked shall be turned into hell, and all the nations that forget God." When Israel forgot God, God sent an enemy, a pagan army and a pagan king, to destroy His own house where they were meeting together.

We first meet Daniel when he is about nineteen. He's in captivity. He will later be known as the prophet of the "Times of the Gentiles." The only prophet who refers to Jesus Christ as the Messiah is Daniel. So when Jesus came on the scene, people knew to look for the Messiah, the Anointed of God. The only prophet to give us a panoramic view of world history—from the days of Nebuchadnezzar to the revelation of Jesus Christ in kingdom glory, to establish His kingdom upon the earth—is Daniel.

The "Times of the Gentiles" began with the destruction of Jerusalem in 586 B.C. We are now living in that period, which is paralleled by another period similar in name, the "Fullness of the Gentiles." The "Fullness of the Gentiles" began with the offering of the Gospel of our Lord to the Gentiles. This happened when the Jews rejected Jesus Christ and the Gospel. It will end at the rapture. But the "Times of the Gentiles" will not end until Jesus comes to establish His kingdom upon the earth. Jesus Himself said, "Jerusalem shall be trodden down of the Gentiles until the times of the Gentiles be fulfilled" (Luke 21:24).

We seem to be coming close to that hour. The rapture seems close at hand—then the Tribulation, then the revelation of Christ and the end of that period, the "Times of the Gentiles."

Daniel means "judged of God." His ministry ran from 606 B.C. (the time he was taken into captivity) until 533 B.C.—more than seventy years. His life somewhat parallels that of Joseph. Remember, Joseph was exalted as the second ruler in all of Egypt. Daniel was exalted as the Prime Minister of the great Babylonian Empire, second only to the king.

What a life! what a man! what an example! what a prophet! what a preacher! what a spokesman for God! Daniel is known as the chronologer, the historian, the politician among the prophets.

I. SOURCE OF DANIEL'S WISDOM

Look at verse 17: "As for these four children . . ."—just youngsters, teenagers.

Young people, God has a place for you to serve. Don't think that, because you are not twenty-one or thirty-one or forty-one or fifty-one, you cannot serve God. You can! In fact, records and statistics show that most people who are saved, are saved before they are fifteen. God needs teenagers like you, teenagers who will determine to serve Him. God needs young girls who will determine to preserve their virginity until married. God needs young men who will dare to be clean, pure and wholesome and not take advantage of the opposite sex. Fellows, listen to me! Don't try to pull that old stunt, "Prove your love to me." That's as old as Adam.

Parents, see to it that your children run with the right crowd. Whom they date, they will sooner or later choose as a mate. This is a serious matter, and I could not fulfill my pastoral duty to you if I didn't tell you to do right, live right, think right, act right, be right. When you walk down this aisle to say, "I do," be able to say it as one pure and clean.

Daniel and his companions were only teenagers, but God had a place in history for a teenager who said, "I will not"!

Where did they get this wisdom? From God. Back to verse 17: "God gave them knowledge and skill in all learning and wisdom."

I read this in James 1:5–8:

"If any of you lack wisdom, let him ask of God, that giveth to all men liberally, and upbraideth not; and it shall be given him. But let him ask in faith, nothing wavering. For he that wavereth is like a wave of the sea driven with the wind and tossed. For let not that man think that he shall receive any thing of the Lord. A double minded man is unstable in all his ways."

Set your mind singularly to believe God, to trust God, to put your faith in God, to put your life in His hands; for He is the God of wisdom.

Proverbs 9:8 reads, "Reprove not a scorner, lest he hate thee: rebuke a wise man, and he will love thee." If you are wise, you will love your pastor for rebuking you for your sins. Love the man of God who stands up and tells you what is right and wrong in the light of God's Word. If you don't love him, the Bible calls you a fool.

"Reprove not a scorner [a fool], *lest he hate thee: rebuke a wise man, and he will love thee. Give instruction to a wise man, and he will be yet wiser: teach a just man, and he will increase in learning. The fear of the Lord is the beginning of wisdom: and the knowledge of the holy is understanding."*—Prov. 9:8–10.

Get it straight: Wisdom comes out of the Bible, not out of magazines, not out of tapes, not out of bookstores. You'll not get wisdom in the classroom nor from the university professor. One gets wisdom from God, the Author of all wisdom.

Daniel's Teacher was God (Isa. 48:17): "I am the Lord thy God which teacheth thee . . . ." Daniel's text was the Word of God (Ps. 119:11): "Thy word have I hid in mine heart, that I might not sin against thee." Daniel's tuition was the resources of God.

> **My Father is rich in houses and lands,**
> **He holdeth the wealth of the world in His hands!**
> **Of rubies and diamonds, of silver and gold,**
> **His coffers are full, He has riches untold.**

Quit bad-mouthing; quit telling everybody God's broke. Get hold of the spout, get in on God's cycle of giving; then see what He will do for you. It will shock you to see how He can meet your needs. He'll pay your tuition all through life if you will trust Him.

II. SCOPE OF DANIEL'S WISDOM

What kind of wisdom did this man have? Was he just an ordinary "Johnny-Come-Lately" who fell off a turnip truck awhile ago? Verse 20 says he was "ten times better [smarter] than all the magicians and astrologers . . . ." That's going some, since the wise men of Babylon were known for their wisdom. The Chaldeans were the smartest people on earth. Daniel was better "in all matters of wisdom and understanding"—ten times better.

Where did it start? I believe at his mother's knee.

You parents, don't depend on the pastor and the schoolteacher to teach your children all they need to know. Give it to them at home. You have them much longer than I have them. You have them much longer than the Sunday school teacher has them. Take time for them even in your busy schedule. Get up a little earlier or stay up a little later or cut out a TV program or quit reading your magazines for awhile, and teach your children about God. Dedicate them to God. Teach them the ways of the Lord. Then when they are older, they will not depart from it. It didn't say they wouldn't stray from it—most of them will—but later on they will not depart from it. Take that to the bank, because God said it.

Look back at verse 5. Daniel and his friends had a three-year course. Three years they were put through the test. They studied. They came to the final exam in verse 19: "...therefore stood they before the king..."—final exam day. And guess what! The king found them fleshier, fairer, wiser and smarter than all the wise men of Babylon.

God gave them wisdom, wisdom broader than the wisdom of all the men of Babylon.

III. SHOWING OF DANIEL'S WISDOM

First, we saw the source—God. Then the scope—wiser than all the wise men.

How did Daniel show how smart he really was?

1. *By his physical appearance.* A healthy body can be a great asset. Keeping one's self clean is important.

I read a story about two men sitting by each other. One said, sniffing, "I believe you use deodorant." The other said, sniffing, "I believe you don't."

Keep a clean, healthy body. Watch what you eat, because what you eat, you are.

Daniel and his companions just ate beans and water. Surely those beans must have been peanuts. I'm trying to find a translation that says they were. But whatever it was they ate, it was not the meat and the wine of the king. Yet they fared better and looked better.

Daniel showed how smart he was by his physical appearance. After all, the body is the temple of the Holy Spirit. So we each ought to look like a Christian, smell like a Christian, walk like a Christian, talk like a Christian and act like a Christian. Physical appearance is important.

2. *By his spiritual dedication.* Verse 8: "Daniel purposed in his heart that he would not defile himself. . . ." In talking about spiritual dedication, remember this: Daniel was in a strange place, 700 or 800 miles from home.

Ever notice how some people act when they get away from home? Daniel could have drunk all the wine he could hold. Without a newspaper or television or telegraph stations, nobody back home would have heard about it. But Daniel had character. And character is what you will do even if you know nobody in the world will ever know about it. Daniel was among foreigners, in a strange place. He had the pull of the youth of Babylon, who said to him, "Come on; let's get drunk."

Out there in your world are those who want you to do the same thing. Sometimes the hardest word in the English language to say is the word NO. But you had better learn how to say it to drink, to drugs, to sex, to gambling, to stealing, to cheating, to lying and to all the rest; or a few years down the line you'll be back saying to me, "Pastor, I wish I had listened to you; then I wouldn't have sold my virginity for one night's pleasure" or "I wouldn't have burned my brain on drugs and dope" or "I wouldn't have gone down the highway in a drunken stupor, had a wreck and killed a man, pastor." Yes, then you will wish you had listened.

You can go into a strange country or off to the army or away to college or sail to another land, but a myrtle tree is a myrtle tree, even in the middle of the desert. A Christian is a Christian wherever he goes. Geography does not change one's behavior.

Young men, don't be blinded by the bright lights of Babylon.

Stick with the right. When I was a student at Bob Jones University almost forty years ago, so often Dr. Bob Jones, Sr., preached to the students, "Do right though the stars fall."

Daniel was in a strange place, among strange, pagan people.

In verse 7 we see these people had a strange procedure: they brainwashed these four young men. The first part of brainwashing in Babylon was changing Daniel's name. Daniel meant "judged of Jehovah"; so they changed his name to Belteshazzar, meaning "a prince favored by the god Baal." They brainwashed him—this young man in a strange place, among strange people, and now with a strange name.

But wait! Daniel said NO. Verse 8: "But Daniel purposed in his heart that he would not defile himself with the portion of the king's meat, nor with the wine which he drank: therefore he requested...."

See how he remained a gentleman—"he requested."

A Christian can also be a gentleman. I've seen a lot of them not act like gentlemen. Some get mad, fly off the handle, tell somebody off in a store and leave a bad testimony. Five dollars, ten dollars, fifty dollars—no amount of money is worth your testimony. Keep your cool. Be a gentleman. Show people that a Christian can be an upright citizen and be kind, compassionate and honorable.

Daniel "requested." He didn't demand of the authorities that he not eat that meat nor drink that wine.

Most people of the world will respect our stand for God. They may not show it right then, but later they will pat us on the back and say, "I appreciate your convictions." They may never agree with your philosophy, but they have to appreciate your stand.

Daniel vowed not to do it. He "purposed in his heart that he would not defile himself...." Daniel could handle lions when he was ninety because he learned how to handle temptation when he was nineteen.

His is the way to do it. Don't wait until you are seventy-five to start living for God. If you're not living for Him now, young people, you will not be living for God five years or ten years from now. The going will get harder, not easier.

Daniel learned to say NO.

Physical appearance, his spiritual dedication and his emotional stability.

I see in verses 11 to 13 that, in the midst of a pagan society, Daniel exercised restraint. In *character*, he was firm and flawless. In *conviction*, he was forceful. In *courage*, he was fearless. In *courtesy*, he was fraternal. Daniel was a gentleman. He went to school in Babylon and graduated with a diploma signed by the king. Before his story ends, even the king himself will know Daniel's God.

You, too, can influence others.

Have character, conviction, be courteous, stand courageously for God; and you will be characterized as the smartest man in town.

──── *Outline* 2:1–18 ────

The Forgotten Dream

Introduction

Status of Daniel
Situation in Babylon
Scene in the palace

Message

I. THE FORGOTTEN DREAM—verse 5

NOTE: God uses dreams when dreams are necessary—Job 33:13–17.

But within the framework of the Bible—since we have the full and final revelation of God.
- Dreams are no longer necessary.
- Jeremiah 23:25–32

NOTE: God has spoken—Heb. 1:1–3.

NOTE: *"More sure word of prophecy"* (II Pet. 1:17–19)

NOTE: The Word of God is:
- Pure—Psalm 119:140—*"Thy word is very pure."*
- Perfect—Psalm 19:7—*"The law of the Lord is perfect...."*
- Powerful—Hebrews 4:12
- Permanent—Psalm 119:89
- Profitable—II Timothy 3:16

QUESTION: How does a forgotten dream affect a person?
What about King Nebuchadnezzar?

II. THE FRUSTRATED WISE MEN—verses 7–11

NOTE: Worldly wisdom devilish—James 3:15

NOTE: Those who are "worldly" wise are usually "heavenly" foolish.

NOTE: Human reason always fails to lay hold on divine wisdom.
- Everything is dark without divine illumination.
- Only Word of God can bring light, understanding—Psalm 119:130.

NOTE: Path of earthly glory leads only to grave—verse 12b.

III. THE FURIOUS KING—verses 12, 13

NOTE: Anger, characteristic of a fool—Ecclesiastes 7:9
- Proverbs 14:17
- Proverbs 22:24
- Ephesians 4:26
- Proverbs 19:11

NOTE: Anger drives man to irrational decisions (text: classic example).

NOTE: King's anger vented toward Daniel—verse 13
Mistake to think he can destroy God's servants
- Psalm 105:15—*"Touch not. . . ."*

NOTE: Daniel/companions: On different wavelengths; belonged to different clan

IV. THE FEARLESS PROPHET—verse 16

NOTE: Daniel feared God:
- Psalm 118:8

> **NOTE:** Daniel feared God (cont.)
> - Psalm 119:74
> - Proverbs 3:7, 8
> - Ecclesiastes 12:13
>
> **NOTE:** He who fears God need not fear man.
> - Luke 12:4, 5
>
> **NOTE:** Why should we fear?
> We have the assurance of God's protection at all times, under all circumstances:
> - Isaiah 41:10—*"Fear thou not...."*
> - Hebrews 13:6—*"I will not fear what man...."*
> - Psalm 27:1—*"The Lord is my light...."*
> - Psalm 118:6—*"The Lord is on my side; I will not fear: What can man do unto me?"*

V. THE FAITHFUL FEW—verses 17, 18

> **NOTE:** God always has a faithful minority:
> - Gideon's 300
> - Joshua 23:10—*"One man of you shall chase a thousand."*
> - Romans 8:31—*"If God be for us...."*
>
> **NOTE:** God never requires greatness; He only requires faithfulness.
> - Revelation 2:10
> - Matthew 25:23—*"Well done...."*
> - Luke 16:10—*"He that is faithful in that which is least is faithful also in much."*
>
> **NOTE:** These four got together for a "cottage prayer meeting."
> 1. They prayed to God for mercy.
> 2. They prayed believing.
> 3. They prayed fervently—James 5:16.
> 4. They prayed for something specific.

NOTE: Daniel knew the faithfulness of God:
- Psalm 37:4, 5
- Lamentations 3:22, 23

NOTE: Matthew 18:19, 20

CHAPTER TWO

The Forgotten Dream

1. *And in the second year of the reign of Nebuchadnezzar Nebuchadnezzar dreamed dreams, wherewith his spirit was troubled, and his sleep brake from him.*

2. *Then the king commanded to call the magicians, and the astrologers, and the sorcerers, and the Chaldeans, for to shew the king his dreams. So they came and stood before the king.*

3. *And the king said unto them, I have dreamed a dream, and my spirit was troubled to know the dream.*

4. *Then spake the Chaldeans to the king in Syriack* [or the ancient Aramaic language in which part of Daniel, from chapter 2, verse 4, through chapter 7, was written. They spake to him in the Syriack language.]*, O king, live for ever: tell thy servants the dream, and we will shew the interpretation.*

5. *The king answered and said to the Chaldeans, The thing is gone from me: if ye will not make known unto me the dream, with the interpretation thereof, ye shall be cut in pieces, and your houses shall be made a dunghill.*

6. *But if ye shew the dream, and the interpretation thereof, ye shall receive of me gifts and rewards and great honour: therefore shew me the dream, and the interpretation thereof.*

7. *They answered again and said, Let the king tell his servants the dream, and we will shew the interpretation of it.*

8. *The king answered and said, I know of certainty that ye would gain the time, because ye see the thing is gone from me.*

9. *But if ye will not make known unto me the dream, there is but one decree for you: for ye have prepared lying and corrupt words to speak before me, till the time be changed: therefore tell me the dream, and I shall know that ye can shew me the interpretation thereof.*

10. *The Chaldeans answered before the king, and said, There is not a man upon the earth that can shew the king's matter: therefore there is no king, lord, nor ruler, that asked such things at any magician, or astrologer, or Chaldean.*

11. *And it is a rare thing that the king requireth, and there is none other that can shew it before the king, except the gods, whose dwelling is not with flesh.*

12. *For this cause the king was angry and very furious, and commanded to destroy all the wise men of Babylon.*

13. *And the decree went forth that the wise men should be slain; and they sought Daniel and his fellows to be slain.*

14. *Then Daniel answered with counsel and wisdom to Arioch the captain of the king's guard, which was gone forth to slay the wise men of Babylon:*

15. *He answered and said to Arioch the king's captain, Why is the decree so hasty from the king? Then Arioch made the thing known to Daniel.*

16. *Then Daniel went in, and desired of the king that he would give him time, and that he would shew the king the interpretation.*

17. *Then Daniel went to his house, and made the thing known to Hananiah, Mishael, and Azariah, his companions:*

18. *That they would desire mercies of the God of heaven concerning this secret; that Daniel and his fellows should not*

perish with the rest of the wise men of Babylon.—Dan. 2:1–18.

Quite a story, wouldn't you say? Where would we look for something like this except within the annals of Scripture?

Daniel is now held captive. You remember that in 606 B.C., when Nebuchadnezzar and the armies of Babylon marched against Jerusalem in the first of three attacks against the holy city, young Daniel was captured and taken to Babylon where he would prove himself worthy. In fact, Daniel was ten times smarter than all the wise men of Babylon.

The situation is an uneasy one. The king is bloodthirsty. He has now dreamed a dream. In the palace is concern at what may happen next, for the king has forgotten his dream. In those days and in that culture, much stock was placed in dreams.

My message today is about

I. THE FORGOTTEN DREAM

Verse 5 says, "The king answered and said to the Chaldeans, The thing is gone from me." In other words, "I have forgotten the dream."

Let me say that God may use dreams when necessary. In Job, chapter 33, Job is being comforted by one of his comforters—if you can call him that. In verses 13 through 17 there is a reference to dreams:

"Why dost thou strive against him? for he giveth not account of any of his matters. For God speaketh once, yea twice, yet man perceiveth it not. In a dream, in a vision of the night, when deep sleep falleth upon men, in slumberings upon the bed; Then he openeth the ears of men, and sealeth their instruction, That he may withdraw man from his purpose, and hide pride from man."

What is this passage about? It is saying to us that, before the Bible was written, God spoke to men through dreams. Now that we have full revelation of God within the Bible, dreams are no longer necessary.

I don't put stock in anybody who tells me God gave him a dream and he wants me to believe God has revealed something special to him, when God has already revealed it in His Word.

Please don't misunderstand me. I can't control your dreams nor my own. But God is not now revealing His will or plan or program or prophecy to men in dreams. He has already revealed Himself within the framework of His Word.

Jeremiah 23 gives a classic example that God does not now give men messages in dreams.

"I have heard what the prophets said, that prophesy lies in my name, saying, I have dreamed, I have dreamed. How long shall this be in the heart of the prophets that prophesy lies? yea, they are prophets of the deceit of their own heart; Which think to cause my people to forget my name by their dreams which they tell every man to his neighbour, as their fathers have forgotten my name for Baal. The prophet that hath a dream, let him tell a dream; and he that hath my word, let him speak my word faithfully. What is the chaff to the wheat? saith the Lord. [The dream means nothing more than chaff to wheat. The real meat is in the wheat.] *Is not my word like as a fire? saith the Lord; and like a hammer that breaketh the rock in pieces? Therefore, behold, I am against the prophets, saith the Lord, that steal my words every one from his neighbour. Behold, I am against the prophets, saith the Lord, that use their tongues, and say, He saith. Behold, I am against them that prophesy false dreams, saith the Lord, and do tell them, and cause my people to err by their lies, and by their lightness; yet I sent them not, nor commanded them: therefore they shall not profit this people at all, saith the Lord."*—Vss. 25-32.

I repeat: there was a time when God used dreams, but now

He has a more specific Word—the Bible. God has spoken. God is still speaking now, but speaking out of His Word, through His servants, by the Holy Spirit.

"God, who at sundry times and in divers manners spake in time past unto the fathers by the prophets, Hath in these last days spoken unto us by his Son [God never spoke more clearly than when He spoke by His Son], *whom he hath appointed heir of all things, by whom also he made the worlds; Who being the brightness of his glory, and the express image of his person, and upholding all things by the word of his power, when he had by himself purged our sins, sat down on the right hand of the Majesty on high."*—Heb. 1:1–3.

The Bible is written. The revelation is full, final, complete. God is not going to allow anybody to add to it or take away from it.

In II Peter, chapter 1, is an amazing passage. To know how God rates the Bible, listen to this, beginning at verse 17:

"For he [Jesus Christ] *received from God the Father honour and glory, when there came such a voice to him from the excellent glory, This is my beloved Son, in whom I am well pleased. And this voice which came from heaven we heard, when we were with him in the holy mount. We have also a more sure word of prophecy; whereunto ye do well that ye take heed, as unto a light that shineth in a dark place, until the day dawn, and the day star arise in your hearts: Knowing this first, that no prophecy of the scripture is of any private interpretation. For the prophecy came not in old time by the will of man: but holy men of God spake as they were moved by the Holy Ghost."*—Vss. 17–21.

Peter is saying, "We heard God speak from Heaven saying about Jesus, 'This is my beloved Son. Listen to Him'; but we now have a more sure word of prophecy, the Bible, given by inspiration to men as they wrote in days of old." Nothing is more important. No authority above this authority. A sure word of prophecy. "Thy word is very pure," declares Psalm 119:140. And Psalm 19:7 says, "The law of the Lord is perfect, converting the soul: the testimony of the Lord is sure, making wise the simple."

"For the word of God is quick, and powerful, and sharper than any twoedged sword, piercing even to the dividing asunder of soul and spirit, and of the joints and marrow, and is a discerner of the thoughts and intents of the heart."—Heb. 4:12.

Not only is the Word of God pure, perfect and powerful; but it is permanent: "For ever, O Lord, thy word is settled in heaven" (Ps. 119:89).

It is also profitable: "All scripture is given by inspiration of God, and is profitable for doctrine, for reproof, for correction, for instruction in righteousness" (II Tim. 3:16).

Pure, perfect, powerful, permanent, profitable is the Word of God. We don't need some prophet in Arkansas or out in California or somewhere else, giving us some special revelation through a dream. God is not now working in that manner, but He is working through His Word.

Here a man has a dream, and he has forgotten it. Nebuchadnezzar—how did it affect him?

II. THE FRUSTRATED WISE MEN

These frustrated wise men didn't know what to make of this. They said to the king a second and third time, "Tell us your dream, and we will interpret it." But they had become frustrated because they couldn't tell the king what he had dreamed.

They were wise. In fact, of all the men on earth, the Chaldeans, or the Babylonians, were the wisest. But worldly wisdom is devilish. "This wisdom descendeth not from above, but is earthly, sensual, devilish" (James 3:15).

Human reasoning always fails to lay hold on divine wisdom.

Everything is dark without divine illumination. Only the Bible can bring light and understanding. We see from Psalm 119:130, "The entrance of thy words giveth light; it giveth understanding unto the simple."

How are we going to know? From the Bible. The very coming in of the Word of God brings us light, illumination and understanding. All other wisdom is devilish, sensual, earthly.

Someone has said, "The path of earthly glory leads only to the grave."

These wise men, the wisest in Babylon, were under a death sentence.

Our wisdom falls far short when it comes to pleasing and serving God. These wise men were frustrated, to say the least, because the king demanded of them something worldly wisdom cannot produce.

III. THE FURIOUS KING

How did it affect the king? It angered him that the wise men could not give him the interpretation of his dream. "For this cause the king was angry and very furious, and commanded to destroy all the wise men of Babylon. And the decree went forth that the wise men should be slain..." (vss. 12,13).

What did they do? They went for Daniel and his companions, who also were numbered among the wise men of Babylon.

An angry king! Anger is characteristic of a fool. Ecclesiastes 7:9 says so: "Be not hasty in thy spirit to be angry: for anger resteth in the bosom of fools."

Tell me what makes you mad, and I'll know what kind of person you are. Now some things ought to make us mad. But just getting mad for the sake of getting mad poisons the system. "Anger resteth in the bosom of fools." Proverbs 14:17 says, "He that is soon angry dealeth foolishly." Proverbs 22:24: "Make no friendship with an angry man." Ephesians 4:26: "...let not the sun go down upon your wrath." And Proverbs 19:11: "The discretion of a man deferreth his anger."

If one thinks about it, likely he will not get too mad. Anger drives one to do irrational things. Did you ever see a man get mad and knock holes in a wall? or tear up furniture? People do do that. Anger drives one to do irrational things. My text is a classic example. It was totally irrational for a king to demand such a thing. And when his men could not interpret his dream, he became angry enough to put them to death.

The king's anger was also vented toward Daniel, by the way, as we see in verse 13: "And the decree went forth that the wise men should be slain; and they sought Daniel and his fellows to be slain." But Psalm 105:15 warns us, "Touch not mine anointed, and do my prophets no harm."

Did the king really believe he could destroy the man of God, the servant of God, the prophet of God? "Touch not mine anointed." Daniel and his companions, though classified among the wise men, were on a different wavelength. They were plugged up to Heaven's wisdom. They got their knowledge, their wisdom from above—wisdom that is pure, peaceable, easy to be entreated, gentle—wisdom that knows how to discern right from wrong. Their wisdom was from above. They belonged to a different clan. The king could not destroy the prophets of God.

IV. THE FEARLESS PROPHET

Verse 16: "Then Daniel went in, and desired of the king [only a fearless man would do this] that he would give him time, and that he would shew the king the interpretation."

Daniel feared God. What is one of America's problems? That we don't have much fear of God anymore. But Daniel did. Psalm 118:8 reads, "It is better to trust in the Lord than to put confidence in man." Fearing God means trusting God, having a holy reverence for God, standing in awe of God and the Bible. Daniel had that fear of God.

Psalm 119:74 says, "They that fear thee will be glad...." They who fear God are happy.

We read in Proverbs 3:7,8, "Be not wise in thine own eyes: fear the Lord, and depart from evil. It shall be health to thy navel, and marrow to thy bones." Trusting God reverently helps one enjoy better health, says the Book.

Ecclesiastes 12:13 sums it up: "Let us hear the conclusion of the whole matter: Fear God, and keep his commandments: for this is the whole duty of man." The beginning of knowledge is the fear of God, knowing who He is, what He is all about, and what He is up to.

And you know what! If we fear God, we don't have to fear man.

Turn to Luke 12. Jesus gives us a word along that line, in verses 4 and 5. Jesus, our highest authority, is speaking: "And I say unto you my friends, Be not afraid of them that kill the body, and after that have no more that they can do. But I will forewarn you whom ye shall fear: Fear him, which after he hath killed hath power to cast into hell; yea, I say unto you, Fear him."

Fear God, and we need not fear the wrath of man. Why should we fear man anyway, when we have the assurance of God's protection at all times and under all circumstances? Read it in the Bible. Isaiah 41:10 tells us, "Fear thou not; for I am with thee: be not dismayed; for I am thy God: I will strengthen thee; yea, I will help thee; yea, I will uphold thee with the right hand of my righteousness." Listen to Hebrews 13:6 where Paul says, "I will not fear what man shall do unto me." Another word on this is in Psalm 27:1, "The Lord is my light and my salvation; whom shall I fear? the Lord is the strength of my life; of whom shall I be afraid?" Now watch this verse, Psalm 118:6: "...The Lord is on my side; I will not fear." Then David asks a question, "...what can man do unto me?" When we fear and trust God, we don't have to fear what man can do to us. God has given us His Word.

Let's review what Jesus said in Luke 12: "Be not afraid of them that kill the body. . . . Fear him, which, after he hath killed hath power to cast into hell."

A holy reverence of God is desperately needed in this hour.

V. THE FAITHFUL FEW

Finally, let us look at verses 17 and 18. Here we read how Daniel called his companions to prayer. (Aren't you glad we have some with whom we can pray?) One of the most important battlefields we have in our Outreach Army is the prayer battlefield.

"Then Daniel went to his house, and made the thing known to Hananiah, Mishael, and Azariah, his companions: That they would desire mercies of the God of heaven concerning this secret; that Daniel and his fellows should not perish with the rest of the wise men of Babylon."

The faithful few, Daniel and his companions, went home and had a cottage prayer meeting.

There will always be the faithful few. Remember Gideon's three hundred. They started with 32,000, then narrowed down to three hundred. Joshua 23:10 informs us, "One man of you shall chase a thousand." And there is that word of comfort in Romans 8:31, "If God be for us, who can be against us?" God never requires greatness of a man, but faithfulness. Listen to what He said in the last book of the Bible: "Fear none of those things which thou shalt suffer: behold, the devil shall cast some of you into prison, that ye may be tried; and ye shall have tribulation ten days: be thou faithful unto death, and I will give thee a crown of life" (Rev. 2:10).

The faithful few. I want to be numbered among them. Do you? The majority are forgetting God. The majority of Christians are out on pleasure trips or sitting home watching television. They are not interested in what I have to say tonight. Oh, no! They are out having what they call fun. I'm talking about Christians, members of this church.

Don't you want to be numbered among the faithful few who are sold out to God? In Matthew 25:23 Jesus said, "Well done, good and faithful servant; thou hast been faithful over a few things, I will make thee ruler over many things." God measures greatness by faithfulness—Luke 16:10: "He that is faithful in that which is least is faithful also in much."

Daniel and his three companions decided to have a prayer meeting. They prayed believing, they prayed fervently, and they prayed for something specific. Daniel knew the faithfulness of God. Do you? Can you say with the psalmist, "Delight thyself also in the Lord: and he shall give thee the desires of thine heart. Commit thy way unto the Lord; trust also in him; and he shall bring it to pass" (Ps. 37:4,5)?

It would surprise us what God would do if only a few members of Worth Baptist Church got together and prayed until the power of God came.

Charles H. Spurgeon, at the great Spurgeon Tabernacle in London, England, preached to some six thousand at every service and before microphones and loudspeaker systems came into existence. When people from all over the world came into London, one place they always wanted to visit was Spurgeon's Tabernacle.

One day a group of Americans (Americans are very inquisitive) said to the custodian of the Spurgeon Tabernacle, "This is a huge building. We don't understand your power system. Where do you get all this power?"

He said, "If you'll follow me to the basement—this was Saturday—I'll show you where the powerhouse is."

They tiptoed down into the basement and found four hundred men on their knees. The custodian said, "This is our power.

Every Saturday these four hundred come to this church and pray all day for their pastor to preach with power on Sunday."

Why is there not much power in the pulpit today? Because there is little praying in the pew. "Praying pews and powerful pulpits make perfect partners." People don't get anything out of the service because they don't put anything into the service.

If I announced an all-day prayer meeting, from 8:00 a.m. until 6:00 p.m. next Saturday, how many of you would show up? You say, "Oh, we're living in a different age." I know—and that is why we don't have power. We've succumbed to the age in which we live. We've allowed the world to plan our services for us. We have services when the world's not having something going on. We're making everything comfortable and convenient for people.

We'll never see great things happening until we learn to sacrifice for God.

Do you want a revival? Then get on your knees and start praying. A fellow asked me the other day, "Pastor, what can I do for revival?" I answered, "Just pray. Prayer is where the power is."

These four young fellows got together to pray. They prayed for mercy. They prayed that God would do something. They prayed specifically. They prayed believing. Daniel knew the faithfulness of God. He knew what Lamentations 3:22, 23 said: "It is of the Lord's mercies that we are not consumed, because his compassions fail not. They are new every morning: great is thy faithfulness."

Two verses of Scripture that could change everything in this church are Matthew 18:19 and 20. Just do what Jesus said do in this prescription: ". . . if two of you shall agree on earth as touching any thing that they shall ask, it shall be done for them of my Father which is in heaven. For where two or three [not two or three dozen, not two or three hundred, not two or three thousand—'where two or three'] are gathered together in my name, there am I in the midst of them."

There Is a God in Heaven

Introduction

Daniel, a man of faith:

- He believed that God would answer prayer; do you?
- God always answers prayer—Jeremiah 33:3.
- Only time God is **deaf** is when we are **dumb**.
- Only time God doesn't **answer** is when we don't **ask**.
- Promise of Jesus—Matthew 7:7–11—*"Ask, and it shall...."*

NOTE: Recall "prayer meeting"—verses 17, 18.

NOTE: Somewhere between verses 18 and 19, Daniel went home, went to bed, went to sleep.
- Reason we can sleep: God never does—Psalm 121.
- Psalm 4:8—*"I will both lay me down and sleep."*
- Psalm 127:2—*"... he giveth his beloved sleep."*

NOTE: During the night God revealed the king's dream to Daniel while he slept.

Message

I. THE GOD IN HEAVEN IS GOD AND FATHER OF OUR LORD JESUS CHRIST.
- John 1:1, 2, 14—*"In the beginning...."*
- John 3:16—*"For God so loved...."*
- John 10:30—*"I and my Father are one."*

- John 14:9—"...*he that hath seen me hath seen the Father.*"
- Hebrews 1:1–4—"*God...Hath in these last days spoken unto us by his Son....*"

II. THE GOD IN HEAVEN IS GOD OF WISDOM WHO ALONE IS WORTHY TO BE PRAISED.

NOTE: Verse 19—"*Daniel blessed the God of heaven.*"
- Psalm 150:6—"*Let every thing....*"
- "Praise God from whom all...."

NOTE: Three things keep us from praising God:
1. Fear
2. Timidity
3. Pride
   - Don't be afraid to praise God.
   - Don't be ashamed to praise God.
   - Don't be too proud to praise God.

NOTE: In the wisdom of God (verse 20):
1. He changes times and seasons.
2. He elevates, demotes rulers—Psalm 75:6, 7.
3. He gives wisdom to men—James 1:5.
4. He reveals deep and secret things—verses 22, 28.
   —Psalm 25:14—"*The secret of the Lord is with them that fear him.*"
5. He penetrates the darkness and dwells in light.
   - Darkness cannot hide you from God—Psalm 139:12.
   - God is light—I John 1:5–7: "*This then....*"

III. THE GOD IN HEAVEN IS THE GOD OF ALL POWER.

> **NOTE:** Matthew 28:18–20
>
> Exodus 15:6: *"Thy right hand, O Lord, is become glorious in power."*
>
> 1. Power to save—Hebrews 7:25— *"Wherefore . . ."*
> 2. Power to satisfy—Psalm 107:9—*"He satisfieth . . . the hungry soul."*
> 3. Power to secure—John 10:27–29

Conclusion

The God of Heaven is here now.

CHAPTER THREE

There Is a God in Heaven

19. *Then was the secret revealed unto Daniel in a night vision. Then Daniel blessed the God of heaven.*

20. *Daniel answered and said, Blessed be the name of God for ever and ever: for wisdom and might are his:*

21. *And he changeth the times and the seasons: he removeth kings, and setteth up kings: he giveth wisdom unto the wise, and knowledge to them that know understanding:*

22. *He revealeth the deep and secret things: he knoweth what is in the darkness, and the light dwelleth with him.*

23. *I thank thee, and praise thee, O thou God of my fathers, who hast given me wisdom and might, and hast made known unto me now what we desired of thee: for thou hast now made known unto us the king's matter.*

24. *Therefore Daniel went in unto Arioch, whom the king had ordained to destroy the wise men of Babylon: he went and said thus unto him; Destroy not the wise men of Babylon: bring me in before the king, and I will shew unto the king the interpretation.*

25. *Then Arioch brought in Daniel before the king in haste, and said thus unto him, I have found a man of the captives*

of Judah, that will make known unto the king the interpretation.

26. *The king answered and said to Daniel, whose name was Belteshazzar, Art thou able to make known unto me the dream which I have seen, and the interpretation thereof?*

27. *Daniel answered in the presence of the king, and said, The secret which the king hath demanded cannot the wise men, the astrologers, the magicians, the soothsayers, shew unto the king;*

28. *But there is a God in heaven that revealeth secrets, and maketh known to the king Nebuchadnezzar what shall be in the latter days. Thy dream, and the visions of thy head upon thy bed, are these;*

29. *As for thee, O king, thy thoughts came into thy mind upon thy bed, what should come to pass hereafter: and he that revealeth secrets maketh known to thee what shall come to pass.*

30. *But as for me, this secret is not revealed to me for any wisdom that I have more than any living, but for their sakes that shall make known the interpretation to the king, and that thou mightest know the thoughts of thy heart.*—Dan. 2:19–30.

Verse 28, "But there is a God in heaven...." Daniel was a man of faith. The Bible defines *faith* as "the substance of things hoped for, the evidence of things not seen." If you could see it, it wouldn't be by faith. If you could realize it, visualize it, handle it, touch it, experience it by the senses, either taste, smell, vision, hearing or feeling, then it wouldn't be of faith.

Faith is the *eye* that sees the invisible. Faith is the *ear* that hears the inaudible. Faith is the *hand* that touches the intangible.

Chapter 11 of Hebrews gives us the "Heroes of Faith." One by one God names them. All kinds of people are there. A harlot is in that group, Rahab; by faith she hid the spies. A murderer is in that group; an adulterer is in that group; a proud king is in that group. A lot of people are listed. None deserved anything, but they got everything by faith in the Word of God.

All that we have comes to us through faith in Jesus Christ.

Daniel was a man of faith. Daniel believed that God would answer prayer. Daniel made known his belief when he said, "I thank thee, and praise thee, O thou God of my fathers, who hast given me wisdom and might, and hast made known unto me now what we desired of thee." Daniel is saying, "God, I thank You for answering prayer."

By the way, when did you last thank God for answering your prayer? Are you so busy asking God that you don't take time to thank God for what He has done for you?

Do you believe God answers prayer? I think I ought to tell you that God always answers prayer. Sometimes He says *yes,* sometimes He says *no,* sometimes He says *wait* awhile. But God always answers. Jeremiah 33:3 bids us, "Call unto me, and I will answer thee, and shew thee great and mighty things, which thou knowest not."

God is still in the prayer-answering business. The only time He is *deaf* is when you're *dumb!* The only time He doesn't *answer* is when you don't *ask.* The only time He doesn't *hear* is when you don't *call.* God answers prayer. Jesus made a promise, and Jesus is a Gentleman, and so Jesus keeps His Word.

In Matthew, chapter 7, Jesus said:

"Ask, and it shall be given you; seek, and ye shall find; knock, and it shall be opened unto you: For every one that asketh receiveth; and he that seeketh findeth; and to him that knocketh it shall be opened. Or what man is there of you, whom if his son ask bread, will he give him a stone? Or if he ask a fish, will he give him a serpent? if ye then, being evil, know how to give good gifts unto your children, how much more shall your Father which is in heaven give good things to them that ask him?"—Vss. 7–11.

What parent here would give your child a rock for a piece of bread? Not one. What daddy in this house would give your son a serpent, if he asked you for a hunk of bologna to make a bologna sandwich? Not one.

What I'm saying is, if you being evil will give good things to your children, how much more will your Father in Heaven give good things to them that ask Him?

Remember the prayer meeting they had in verses 17 and 18, when Daniel went to his house and made this request of the king known to his three friends, that they would desire the mercies of the God of Heaven concerning this secret. They called for a prayer meeting and prayed, and God answered their prayer.

Because this is Father's Day, I've been thinking about my daddy today. He went to be with God thirty years ago, but there's hardly a day that I don't miss him, that I don't think about him. Years ago my father had a cancer on his lip. He was driving fifty miles from home to Greensboro, North Carolina, to one of the best hospitals, with the best team of doctors in that part of the country. They had already told him he had cancer and he had to be operated on.

Daddy went to a fellowship meeting. He got a bunch of preachers together, and they got down on their knees and prayed that God would heal my daddy.

The next day he entered Cone Memorial Hospital in Greensboro, North Carolina. They stretched him out to do surgery. But then the doctor came in and said, "What cancer? He doesn't need surgery; send him home."

I tell you, God answers prayer!

When I was twenty-five years old, I was in the hospital room with my daddy on a Saturday night. A man who had been a member of our church for a long time, but who had gotten away from God, had just learned that day that Daddy was very critically ill. He came into the hospital room, got down on his knees by my daddy's bed on Saturday night and prayed, "Dear God, please, please take the years off of my life and put them on my pastor's life because this town needs him." Three days later, my daddy went out of that hospital on crutches and preached that man's funeral.

I'm telling you, God answers prayer! He answers prayer in the morning; He answers prayer at noon; He answers prayer in the evening, so keep your heart in tune.

Between verses 18 and 19, Daniel went home, went to bed and went to sleep. And God revealed the king's dream to Daniel as he slept.

I. GOD AND FATHER OF JESUS CHRIST

My message is entitled "There Is a God in Heaven."

Every time I have an opportunity to sign someone's Bible, I write John 1:1, 2 and 14. These are my life's verses:

"In the beginning was the Word, and the Word was with God, and the Word was God. The same was in the beginning with God. . . . And the Word was made flesh, and dwelt among us, (and we beheld his glory, the glory as of the only begotten of the Father,) full of grace and truth."

Let us read John 3:16, "For God so loved the world, that he gave his only begotten Son, that whosoever believeth in him should not perish, but have everlasting life." Then in John 10:30 Jesus said, "*I* and my Father are one." And He said in John 14:9, "He that hath seen me hath seen the Father." A longer passage is Hebrews 1:1-4:

"God, who at sundry times and in divers manners spake in time past unto the fathers by the prophets, Hath in these last days spoken unto us by his Son, whom he hath appointed heir of all things, by whom also he made the worlds; Who being the brightness of his glory, and the express image of his person,

and upholding all things by the word of his power, when he had by himself purged our sins, sat down on the right hand of the Majesty on high; Being made so much better than the angels, as he hath by inheritance obtained a more excellent name than they."

Who is this God whom Daniel served? Who is this God whom your fathers and mine have served? Who is this God in Heaven? The God and Father of our Lord Jesus Christ.

II. GOD OF WISDOM

The God in Heaven is the God of *wisdom,* who alone is worthy to be praised. Look at verse 19: "Then Daniel blessed the God of heaven."

Says Psalm 103:1, "Bless the Lord, O my soul: and all that is within me, bless his holy name." Then Psalm 150:6 admonishes, "Let every thing that hath breath praise the Lord. Praise ye the Lord."

> **Praise God, from whom all blessings flow;**
> **Praise Him, all creatures here below,**
> **Praise Him above, ye heav'nly hosts;**
> **Praise Father, Son and Holy Ghost.**

Three things keep people from praising God: *fear, timidity* and *pride.*

Somebody says, "If I praise God, I'm afraid they'll call me a fanatic" or "We knew he was kind of strange."

People go to a ball game and holler and scream until they are hoarse and just about to collapse. "Boy, what a *fan* he is!" you will hear them say. That same fellow can go to church and say, "Amen!" and the same people will say, "He's a *fanatic.*" Well, I'd rather restrain a fanatic than raise a corpse any day. Don't be afraid to praise God.

We don't know how to praise God from the depths of our souls. But don't be afraid, don't be timid, don't be too proud, don't be ashamed. Oh, praise Him, praise Him, Jesus our blessed Redeemer!

In verse 20, "Daniel answered and said, Blessed be the name of God for ever and ever: for wisdom and might are his."

The God in Heaven "changeth the times and the seasons," verse 21 tells us. Who is changing the world course of events? God is in control. But you say, "He hasn't done much for me lately." Are you breathing? Are you alive? When I got up this morning, I thanked God I was able to get out of bed. Some people couldn't get out of bed this morning.

I thank God that I can speak to you this morning. If I couldn't preach, I'd be in bad shape. I thank God that I can eat. I thank God that my wife didn't put arsenic in my eggs this morning! (Some wives have done that, you know.)

I thank God that He is in control and has the power to do far above anything that we could ask or think. He changes the times and seasons.

That's not all. In His wisdom, He elevates and demotes the rulers of the nations of earth—verse 21: "He removeth kings, and setteth up kings." Psalm 75:6, 7 also says, "For promotion cometh neither from the east, nor from the west, nor from the south. But God is the judge: he putteth down one, and setteth up another." God is still controlling the nations of earth.

Then He gives wisdom to men—James 1:5,6:

"If any of you lack wisdom, let him ask of God, that giveth to all men liberally, and upbraideth not; and it shall be given him. But let him ask in faith, nothing wavering. For he that wavereth is like a wave of the sea driven with the wind and tossed. For let not that man think that he shall receive any thing of the Lord."

If you pray for rain, carry an umbrella.

One day my dad and I were in the bank in my hometown of Danville, Virginia. The banker was talking to my daddy about the farmers who had come in and had said to him, "We can't meet our notes; we haven't had any rain. We must have rain to grow our crop so we can pay off our bills."

Sitting at the other desk was one of the most liberal preachers in town. An answer to prayer would scare him to death! Daddy said to the president of the bank, "Is it all right if I pray for rain?"

"Well—sure, Brother Barber, go right ahead."

So Daddy, who was walking with a cane at the time, hit that cane up against the counter and said, "Ladies and gentlemen, the president of this bank has given me the authority to offer prayer for rain." Daddy started praying; and so help me, before we got out of there, that liberal preacher almost got drowned getting to his car! I mean the rain came.

God is still on the throne, and He still answers prayer.

God knows how to do it. He sets up one, He takes down another. He changes the seasons and the times. He gives wisdom to men. And He reveals the deep, deep secrets of men, says verse 22. Read it: "He revealeth the deep and secret things." So also says verse 28: "But there is a God in heaven that revealeth secrets." Psalm 25:14 states, "The secret of the Lord is with them that fear him."

If you want to get in on God's secrets, then start trusting Him, believing Him.

God in His wisdom not only changes times and seasons, not only elevates and demotes kings and rulers of the earth, not only gives wisdom, not only reveals the deep secret things of life, but He penetrates the darkness and dwells in the light.

Darkness cannot hide you from God. You may think you can get away in the dark corner of some house somewhere or some room somewhere or some car somewhere or some building somewhere or out in the woods somewhere, but darkness doesn't hide you from God—Psalm 139:12: "Yea, the darkness hideth not from thee; but the night shineth as the day: the darkness and the light are both alike to thee." God doesn't have to look at darkness; it's always light to Him. In fact, we read it in I John 1:5–7:

"This then is the message which we have heard of him, and declare unto you, that God is light, and in him is no darkness at all. If we say that we have fellowship with him, and walk in darkness, we lie, and do not the truth: But if we walk in the light, as he is in the light, we have fellowship one with another, and the blood of Jesus Christ his Son cleanseth us from all sin."

III. GOD OF ALL POWER

God is light; He penetrates darkness. Who is this God in Heaven? The God and Father of our Lord Jesus Christ. Who is this God in Heaven? The God of all wisdom. Who is this God in Heaven? The God of all power.

We are living in a power-crazed world. We want cars with greater horsepower, airplanes with more powerful engines, rockets with more power; we want coffee pots that will brew in thirty seconds. We want power, power, power and more power.

Jesus said in Matthew 28:18, "All power is given unto me in heaven and in earth." Exodus 15:6 tells us, "Thy right hand, O Lord, is become glorious in power."

I've come to tell you tonight that God has power to *save*—Hebrews 7:25: "Wherefore he is able also to save them to the uttermost that come unto God by him." He has power to satisfy—Psalm 107:9: "For he satisfieth the longing soul, and filleth the hungry soul with goodness." And He has power to *secure*. Jesus put it this way, in John 10:27-29:

"My sheep hear my voice, and I know them, and they follow me: And I give unto them eternal life; and they shall never perish, neither shall any man pluck them out of my hand. My

Father, which gave them me, is greater than all; and no man is able to pluck them out of my Father's hand."

The God of Heaven is right here, right now. You don't have to go to Jerusalem to find Him nor make a pilgrimage to Rome to find Him nor hunt up a priest somewhere to find Him. You can find Him right here at this altar of prayer.

> **All hail the power of Jesus' name!**
> **Let angels prostrate fall!**
> **Bring forth the royal diadem,**
> **And crown Him Lord of all.**

The Kingdom Is Coming

Introduction

We have heard many high-sounding platitudes to describe status of national and international affairs:

- Roosevelt had his "New Deal"
- Truman his "Fair Deal"
- Kennedy his "New Society"
- Johnson his "Great Society"
- Reagan his "Reaganomics"
- Bush his "New World Order"

But: None can hold a candle to the "Divine Deal" that will come about when our Commander-in-chief ushers in His worldwide utopia in the millennium.

Message

I. THE IMAGE IN NEBUCHADNEZZAR'S DREAM—verses 31–35

NOTE: Awesome! Terrifying! Terrible!
- Bright countenance
- Terrible form
- Overwhelming appearance

NOTE: Search the annals of history
- Never before a dream like this dream
- Never before such consternation
- Never before adumbration like this

NOTE: Look at huge image:
- What a colossal figure!
- What a head!
- What a body!
- What legs and feet!
  - —No wonder Nebuchadnezzar was fearful and afraid!
  - —No wonder the Wise Men of Babylon shuddered!
  - —No wonder it took divine wisdom to discern meaning and significance of such a colossus!

Description:
- Head—"gold"
- Breast and arms—"silver"
- Belly and thighs—"brass"
- Legs—"iron"
- Toes—"iron and clay"

Observe:
1. The image was that of a man ("Superman").
2. The image contained four metals and clay.
3. The image deteriorated in value from head to toe.

NOTE: Focal point of all this:
- One people—Jews
- One place—Jerusalem

Zechariah 12:1–3
   Verse 3—divided into three parts:

   1. *"Jerusalem, a burdensome stone for all people"*

> **NOTE:** This segment of verse 3 is being fulfilled today.
> - United Nations censures Israel
> - Community of nations against Israel
> - About only reliable ally is United States.
>
> **NOTE:** Quote European reporter:
> "President Reagan trembled when he heard the name Jerusalem."
>
> **NOTE:** All nations have stake in city of Jerusalem.

2. *"All that burden themselves with* [Jerusalem] *shall be cut in pieces."*
   - Jerusalem is a "hot potato" among nations today.
   - No one seems to know what to do with Jerusalem. (Attempts to conduct "peace conference" to settle Arab-Israeli conflict)

> **NOTE:** More than Arabs against Jews—it is the world against Israel.
> - Many nations have already been "cut in pieces" for their treatment of Jerusalem.

3. *"All the people of the earth be gathered against Jerusalem."*

> **NOTE:** This segment of Zechariah 12:3 is about to be fulfilled (Zech 14:2).
>
> **NOTE:** Don't be surprised that Germany has unified (Berlin Wall).
> Don't be surprised that Russia is reaching out to America, Europe, and Asia (Iron Curtain).
> (Worldwide coalition against Israel)

NOTE: Stage being set for Armageddon
All nations against Jews—Jesus intervenes.

QUESTION: Why will every nation or group of nations that
has ever opposed Jerusalem or ever will oppose Jerusalem
ultimately fail?

Why can the U.N. not find acceptable solution to problem
of Jerusalem?

Why is Jerusalem such a "burdensome stone" to all nations?

ANSWER: 1. Jerusalem has a spiritual foundation—(Heb. 11:10).
2. It has experienced what no other city has.
3. It is the eternal capital of Christ's kingdom.
4. It cannot be separated from the King.

NOTE: To fight against Jerusalem is to fight against King
Jesus.

II. THE INTERPRETATION OF DANIEL—verses 36–43

NOTE: Verse 36: *"This is the interpretation."*

1. Head of gold—Babylon (626–536 B.C.)

NOTE: *"God of heaven hath given . . . . "*
(No man has power except what God gives him—
Pilate: John 19:10, 11.)

2. Breast/arms of silver—Medo-Persian (536–331 B.C.)
3. Belly/thighs of brass—Grecian (331–321 B.C.)
4. Legs of iron
Toes of iron/clay—Roman (40 B.C.–A.D. 476)

NOTE: All Gentiles and Gentile powers represented by legs and toes of image, and they all will be a part of the revived Roman Empire led by the Antichrist.

NOTE: In these four empires is found full spectrum of Gentile power from Nebuchadnezzar to present and on to end of "the times of the Gentiles."

(Thus, image in Nebuchadnezzar's dream is a picture of final structure of Gentile power, to be crushed at the revelation of Christ.)

NOTE: This final structure of Gentile power is called "ecclesiastical-political Babylon" (religion and government).

III. THE INTERVENTION OF JESUS—verses 44, 45

NOTE: This is the real "New World Order":
- God's new world
- The millennium
- The kingdom that is coming

NOTE: "Stone"—Jesus/Matthew 21:42–44
1. Saving Stone—I Peter 2:6–8
2. Foundation Stone—Matthew 16:18
3. Crushing Stone—verse 45

Conclusion

1. Jesus Christ will destroy Babylonian system of government which began with Tower of Babel and has continued until its globalized form in these last days.

2. He will bring the nations to the *"winepress of the wrath of God"* (Rev. 19:5).

3. He will rule nations with rod of iron in glorious new world order.

CHAPTER FOUR

The Kingdom Is Coming

There is no book more timely for the hour than the book of Daniel.

Today we begin at Daniel 2:31 and following, as we continue in the series, *A Dozen Diamonds From Daniel.*

31.   *Thou, O king, sawest, and behold a great image. This great image, whose brightness was excellent, stood before thee; and the form thereof was terrible.*

32.   *This image's head was of fine gold, his breast and his arms of silver, his belly and his thighs of brass,*

33.   *His legs of iron, his feet part of iron and part of clay.*

34.   *Thou sawest till that a stone was cut out without hands, which smote the image upon his feet that were of iron and clay, and brake them to pieces.*

35.   *Then was the iron, the clay, the brass, the silver, and the gold, broken to pieces together, and became like the chaff of the summer threshingfloors; and the wind carried them away, that no place was found for them: and the stone that smote the image became a great mountain, and filled the whole earth.*

36.   *This is the dream; and we will tell the interpretation thereof before the king.*

37. *Thou, O king, art a king of kings; for the God of heaven hath given thee a kingdom, power, and strength, and glory.*

38. *And wheresoever the children of men dwell, the beasts of the field and the fowls of the heaven hath he given into thine hand, and hath made thee ruler over them all. Thou art this head of gold.*

39. *And after thee shall arise another kingdom inferior to thee, and another third kingdom of brass, which shall bear rule over all the earth.*

40. *And the fourth kingdom shall be strong as iron: forasmuch as iron breaketh in pieces and subdueth all things: and as iron that breaketh all these, shall it break in pieces and bruise.*

41. *And whereas thou sawest the feet and toes, part of potter's clay, and part of iron, the kingdom shall be divided; but there shall be in it of the strength of the iron, forasmuch as thou sawest the iron mixed with miry clay.*

42. *And as the toes of the feet were part of iron, and part of clay, so the kingdom shall be partly strong, and partly broken.*

43. *And whereas thou sawest iron mixed with miry clay, they shall mingle themselves with the seed of men: but they shall not cleave one to another, even as iron is not mixed with clay.*

44. *And in the days of these kings shall the God of heaven set up a kingdom, which shall never be destroyed: and the kingdom shall not be left to other people, but it shall break in pieces and consume all these kingdoms, and it shall stand for ever.*

45. *Forasmuch as thou sawest that the stone was cut out of the mountain without hands, and that it brake in pieces the iron, the brass, the clay, the silver, and the gold; the great God hath made known to the king what shall come to pass hereafter: and the dream is certain, and the interpretation thereof sure.*

It doesn't take a theologian to know that our world is on a collision course in the early decade of the nineties. Many drastic changes have taken place in the last few years, changes we never dreamed of.

Who would have ever thought that we would have considered joining hands with the Soviet Union, even with Cuba, Germany, Poland, Hungary and all of the Eastern Bloc nations of Europe! We ought not be surprised that the Iron Curtain has been ripped in two. We ought not be surprised that the Berlin Wall came tumbling down. We read and hear of things happening every day that remind us to watch for the coming of our Lord.

The return of Christ is the next major event on God's calendar. We should be thinking of and looking toward that every day. Soon the trumpet will sound. Soon the dead in Christ will rise. Soon those who are alive and remain shall be caught up together with them to meet the Lord in the air, and so shall we ever be with the Lord.

I tell you, our hope is not in Washington nor in our state capital, nor in City Hall nor in the gold or silver reserve nor in the Certificates of Deposit, but in the coming of the Lord.

We've heard all the high-sounding platitudes which describe the status of national and international affairs. Roosevelt had his "New Deal." Truman had, besides Bess, a "Fair Deal." Kennedy had a "New Society" that never amounted to much. Johnson had his "Great Society." Reagan had his "Reaganomics." Bush talked about the "New World Order." But none of these will hold a candle to the "Divine Deal" that will be ushered in by our Commander-in-chief, the Lord Jesus Christ. He it is who will bring peace and prosperity and an economic-political-religious system such as the world has never known.

I've entitled this message "The Kingdom Is Coming." Some good news is on the horizon. Watching television and listening to the radio, we hear lots of bad news. I've never heard anything like it: rape, robbery, burglary, theft, arson, fire, war, famine, pestilence, disease, refugees; people without homes or insurance or food or clothing or family. It's a dark, dismal, discouraging picture.

But there's hope! There's good news! A trumpet is about to sound!

Ladies and gentlemen, I challenge you to live every day as if this could be the last day to see the sun rise. Jesus is coming! The kingdom is coming!

I. THE IMAGE IN NEBUCHADNEZZAR'S DREAM

In this message, there are three things I will talk about. First, the image in Nebuchadnezzar's dream. We read it in verses 31 to 35. This is a most awesome thing, terrifying. The Bible says, ". . . and the form thereof was terrible." This image Daniel saw in his dream had a bright countenance, a terrible form and an overwhelming appearance. Nothing has ever been written like it. Never has there been a dream like Nebuchadnezzar's. Never was there ever such consternation surrounding a dream. Never has there been such an illustration, an adumbration, of what is to come, as we see in these verses.

Look at the huge image. What a colossal figure! What a head! What a body! What legs! What feet! What toes! No wonder Nebuchadnezzar was fearful and afraid. No wonder the men of Babylon shuddered when they thought about it. No wonder the wise men said, 'We don't know what you've dreamed, so how can we tell you what it means?' No wonder it took divine wisdom to decipher and declare the meaning and significance of such a colossus that stood on the plains of Babylon. There has never been anything like it in history.

Look at the head. Daniel said the head is of gold. Look at the breast and arms. Daniel said they are of silver. Look at the belly and thighs. Daniel said they are of brass. Look at the legs. Daniel said they are of iron. Look at the toes. Daniel said they are made of iron mixed with clay.

Observe three things about this image: (1) it was that of a

man—a head, a body, legs, feet; (2) it contained four metals and miry clay; (3) it deteriorated in value.

Watch it! Head of gold—most precious of all metals. Arms and breast of silver—second most precious. Belly and thigh of brass—deteriorating. Legs of iron—deteriorating until the toes become clay. What an awesome thing!

The focal point of every chapter of this book of Daniel and of the Old and New Testaments is the Jew. The focal point geographically is Jerusalem.

Turn to Zechariah, chapter 12. I will read the first three verses, then look at verse 3 a little more closely.

"The burden of the word of the Lord for Israel, saith the Lord, which stretcheth forth the heavens, and layeth the foundation of the earth, and formeth the spirit of man within him. Behold, I will make Jerusalem a cup of trembling unto all the people round about, when they shall be in the siege both against Judah and against Jerusalem. And in that day will I make Jerusalem a burdensome stone for all people: all that burden themselves with it [with Jerusalem] *shall be cut in pieces, though all the people of the earth be gathered together against it* [against Jerusalem]."

Now, I've divided verse 3 into three segments. Two are being fulfilled today; one is yet to be fulfilled.

Segment one—Jerusalem: "And in that day will I make Jerusalem a burdensome stone for all people." This segment is being fulfilled today. Watch your newspapers, listen to the news out of the United Nations. Every chance the United Nations gets, it censors Jerusalem and the nation Israel. The community of nations are against Israel. About the only reliable ally she has is the United States. I pray to God that we will never forsake His people and leave them to the wolves. But there is not a nation on earth that will not sooner or later take a stand against Jerusalem and against Israel. One European reporter said,

"President Reagan trembled when he heard the name Jerusalem." All nations have a stake in that city. I know the last conflict we came through was in Kuwait, but the main target eventually is Jerusalem. It always has been and always will be.

Look at the second part of verse 3: ". . . all that burden themselves with it [Jerusalem] shall be cut in pieces." This also is being fulfilled. Jerusalem is a hot potato among the nations of earth. No one seems to know what to do with her. There are attempts to conduct so-called peace conferences to settle the Arab-Israeli conflict. But no peace conference will ever settle that conflict. Then what will? The Antichrist. He is the strong one the world is looking for. They will bypass the Christ of God and accept the Antichrist.

Many deceiving men shall come and receive accolades, praise and worship. The Stone, the true Stone, is rejected of men. But men will accept the Antichrist. In fact, Israel will make a covenant with him, and he will be their saviour for three and a half years. He will settle the Arab-Israeli conflict. Peace conferences won't do it. Many nations have already been cut in pieces.

Look again at that middle part, that second part: ". . . all that burden themselves with it [Jerusalem] shall be cut in pieces." What am I saying? Many nations have already been cut in pieces for the way they have treated Jerusalem. We could go back to ancient Assyria and Babylon, Rome and Greece, and in modern days, to Germany. All have been cut in pieces because they burdened the city of Jerusalem.

Now the third part of verse 3: ". . . all the people of the earth be gathered together against it." This segment is about to be fulfilled.

Turn a page to Zechariah 14, verses 2, 3:

"For I will gather all nations against [Washington? No. Against Moscow? No. Against London? No.—against] *Jerusalem to*

*battle; and the city shall be taken, and the houses rifled, and
the women ravished; and half of the city shall go forth into captivity, and the residue of the people shall not be cut off from
the city. Then shall the Lord go forth, and fight against those
nations . . . . "*

Every nation will be involved against Jerusalem, and every
nation will have to answer to God for it.

Don't be surprised that Germany is becoming unified again.
Don't be surprised that the Berlin Wall came down. Don't be
surprised that Russia is reaching out to America, Europe and
Asia for aid. Don't be surprised that the Iron Curtain has split
in two. There is a worldwide conspiracy, a worldwide coalition of all nations against Jerusalem. God said it, not me. And
we are nearer that than we have ever been before.

Dear Brother Huffman came this morning, as he does every
Sunday, and said, "Well, pastor, we are one week nearer the
whole thing, aren't we?" Surely it is so.

I've said it before and I say it again: It's dangerous for Christians to miss church. If you miss one Sunday, you will find it
easier to miss the next. You miss a prayer meeting, and it's
easier to miss on Sunday night. You miss on Sunday night, and
it's easier to miss Wednesday night.

The day is approaching; the stage seems to be being set for
Armageddon. All nations will be against the Jews and
Jerusalem.

And what is going to happen? Jesus will intervene. Verse 3
of Zechariah 14 says, "Then shall the Lord go forth, and fight
against those nations . . . . "

Let me ask you this: Why will every nation or group of
nations that fight against Jerusalem or oppose the city of God
ultimately fail? Why can't the United Nations find an adequate
solution to the problem of Jerusalem? Why is she a burdensome stone to all the nations of earth?

There are four reasons.

1. Jerusalem has a spiritual foundation. I read in Hebrews 11:10 that Abraham "looked for a city which hath foundations. . . ." I know he was looking ultimately for Heaven, but he had to find an earthly city first. He was a nomad, a wanderer who lived in tents with Isaac and Jacob, but he looked for a city with a foundation. And no city has one like Jerusalem. It has a spiritual foundation and a material foundation, and Abraham looked for both Jerusalems.

You and I are looking for that heavenly Jerusalem.

2. It has experienced what no other city has experienced. It was in Jerusalem where our Saviour was tried. It was in Jerusalem that they mocked Him. It was in Jerusalem and its environs that they hanged Him upon a cross. It was in Jerusalem where He poured out His blood in behalf of all of Adam's race. It was in the environs of Jerusalem where He arose triumphantly from the dead. No other city has the history that Jerusalem has.

3. It is the eternal capital of Christ's Kingdom on earth. Jesus Christ will literally reign from Jerusalem over all nations. Since the Bible declared it, I don't doubt it. Will it be a literal kingdom? Certainly. On a literal throne? Certainly. Will He be a literal King? Certainly. I believe every word God said. And He said there is coming a literal kingdom upon this earth and that Jesus will reign from Jerusalem to the ends of the earth.

4. Jerusalem cannot be separated from the King. It is His capital. When you oppose Jerusalem, you oppose Christ. When you oppose Jerusalem, fight against Jerusalem, you fight against Christ. The whole spectrum of the image is about what will happen ultimately to Jerusalem.

II. THE INTERPRETATION OF DANIEL

Let's scan verses 36 through 43, for they are so important.

Verse 36 says, "This is the dream...." Daniel is about to tell Nebuchadnezzar what his dream is. Where did Daniel learn what that dream was? He didn't go to a seminar. I'm sick and tired of seminars. I'm getting weary of those who say, "Well, we don't get the answers at church." What's wrong with your hearing? Don't you listen to the preacher? You don't have to go to every Tom, Dick and Harry to find the answers. Listen to your pastor as he expounds the Word of God. Parents, you are getting answers; young people, you are getting answers. Just listen to the Word of God. I'm giving you years of seminar right now, years in one message! If you want to know how to live and how to die, get it out of the Bible. Tune in. Get on the right frequency.

This is the dream and this is the interpretation.

The head of gold—the kingdom of Babylon from the year 626 to the year 536 B.C. and all the kings, namely Nebuchadnezzar, about whom this whole story evolves at this point. Verse 37, "...the God of heaven hath given thee a kingdom...."

Where does man get his power? From God. Remember what Jesus said in John 19:10,11. Remember what He said to Pilate when Pilate said, 'It is in my power to crucify You or to turn You loose. I can set You free, or I can put You to death.' But Jesus replied, 'Mr. Pilate, you have no power but what God gives you.'

Listen, President Yeltsin! Listen, President Clinton. Listen, all ye rulers of the world! You don't have any power that God didn't give you! All power is from God. Jesus said that, and He knew what He was talking about.

Breast and arms of silver—the Media-Persia empire, with Cyrus and Darius the main monarchs there from 536 to 331 B.C. The Medes and Persians ruled the world: first, Babylon, the head of gold; after Babylon, the Medes and Persians, the silver; after the Medes and Persians, the Grecian empire—the belly and thighs of brass, from 331 to 321 B.C.—ten short years.

Alexander the Great conquered the world and spread Hellenism, the Greek culture, throughout the then-known world. The New Testament came in Greek rather than Hebrew or some other language, because Greek was the universal language of that day—not English, but Greek. So the New Testament comes to us in Greek because Alexander spread the Greek culture over the then-known world.

Legs of iron. How do you describe toes of clay and iron mixed together? The Roman Empire reigned from 40 B.C. to about 476 A.D., when it collapsed. What caused the collapse? The same thing that will cause America to collapse—sin. Every nation that sins against God shall be cast into Hell, the Bible declares.

If we love America like we say we love America, we had better start praying that God will do something. If we don't have revival, it will be ruin, damnation, judgment.

Legs of iron—the Roman Empire divided around 325 A.D. into the eastern and western divisions of the empire. It became two. But Rome itself, the city that was the great strength of the Roman Empire, collapsed in 476 A.D. Out of the ruins of that have come all the western bloc of nations: Europe, America and all the rest.

Out of the foundation of the ancient Roman Empire will come the Man of Sin. Every nation in the world is related to the Roman Empire in some way. All Gentiles and all Gentile powers are represented by the legs and toes of the image, and they will be a part of the revived Roman Empire out of which the Antichrist will come.

In these four empires is found the full spectrum of the Gentile power, from Nebuchadnezzar to the present day and up until the day Jesus comes in revelation glory to establish His kingdom on the earth. That is called the "Times of the Gentiles."

The period known as the "Times of the Gentiles" began in 586 B.C., when Nebuchadnezzar overran Jerusalem. Jesus said,

". . . Jerusalem shall be trodden down of the Gentiles, until the times of the Gentiles be fulfilled." That will happen when Jesus comes and destroys the last vestige of Gentile power.

This image in Nebuchadnezzar's dream and Daniel's interpretation of it is a picture of the final structure of Gentile power which is to be crushed at the revelation of Jesus Christ. This is called the "Ecclesiastical-Political Babylon," made up of religion and government joined together.

I repeat: Don't be surprised that Russia and the Soviet Union are reaching out to America and to the Eastern Bloc of European nations, because there is coming this great coalition. And because all nations are against the Jew, against Jerusalem, all nations are anti-God in structure and philosophy of government.

This world is no friend to grace. This world is not going to help you on. Parents, this world is not going to help you rear your children. The humanistic philosophy of education is not going to help you. Only God, the Bible, the Truth will set you free; and whom the Son makes free, he is free indeed.

The image has a head of gold, arms and breast of silver, belly and thighs of brass, legs of iron, toes, some strong and some weak. There are today some strong and some weak nations.

Now remember, Daniel says in verses 34, 35:

"Thou sawest till that a stone was cut out without hands, which smote the image upon his feet that were of iron and clay, and brake them to pieces. Then was the iron, the clay, the brass, the silver, and the gold, broken to pieces together."

In Nebuchadnezzar's dream, the structure of power, the one-world government that is coming together to be headed up by the Antichrist, is symbolized in this image on the plains of Dura, on the plains of Babylon; and only the man of God can give the interpretation of it.

Talk about a divine deal! Talk about a new world order! We are headed that way. And this New Age is not the answer. The

New Age is the old age of humanism dressed up. The New Age is making man his own saviour. The New Age is saying to man, "Look within; you have whatever it takes."

That brings me to another point. I hear preachers talk about building people's self-image. Our image is like filthy rags in God's sight. I'm talking about the unregenerate man now. But you know, some Christians have gotten caught up on this philosophical idea, that we have to improve our image, self-esteem. I have news for you: we don't have any self-esteem. The only esteem we have is in Christ. The only power we have is in Him. The only life we have is in Jesus. He is our only light, our only illumination, our only hope.

Don't read the wrong books. Don't listen to the wrong tapes. Don't go to the wrong source. Go to the Bible. It has the answer on economy. If people would work an honest day, if Christians would tithe—that would straighten out the economy. Then more money could be sent to missionaries, and we could build more Bible schools and churches.

Get your hope and confidence from the Bible. Don't misunderstand me. There are times when we all need enlightenment, when we need somebody to take the Bible and interpret it for us. But we've gone too long after the things of the world.

Even in churches, the humanistic philosophy is being flirted with. I read the other day where one of the leading pastors said, "I don't believe in the deity of Christ nor in the inspiration of the Scripture."

When they want to play up somebody in the news, to whom do they go? To some infidel like him. They are scared of us fundamentalists. They are afraid of the truth. I'm not looking for a newspaper write-up. I'm twenty-five years past that. For the first five years of my ministry, I would hope for a Monday morning call: "What did you preach yesterday?" But I soon found out they don't care what I preached yesterday. I'm not looking for write-ups and a spot on television. I'm looking for the crown that He will have in His hand when He says, 'Well done, good and faithful servant. You have been faithful in preaching the Word. You have been faithful over a few things; I will make you ruler over many things.' The same thing will be true with you and your Sunday school class, with you and your bus route, with you and your choir ministry—wherever you have served—you have been faithful in a few things; then He will make you ruler over many things.

III. THE INTERVENTION OF JESUS

Now Daniel 2:44 and 45: "And in the days of these kings. . . ." What kings? Those toes. Some nations are powerful, some are weak. "And in the days of these kings. . . ." What kings? The kings who will come out of that bloc of power from the revived Roman Empire. "And in the days of these kings. . . ." What is going to happen? The God of Heaven shall set up the greatest kingdom yet to be established. And that kingdom

44. *shall never be destroyed: and the kingdom shall not be left to other people, but it shall break in pieces and consume all these kingdoms, and it shall stand for ever.*

45. *Forasmuch as thou sawest that the stone was cut out of the mountain without hands* [There is the deity of Jesus. There is the virgin birth]*, and that it brake in pieces the iron, the brass, the clay, the silver, and the gold; the great God hath made known to the king what shall come to pass hereafter: and the dream is certain, and the interpretation thereof sure.*"

This is the beginning of the New World order—God's New World order. This is the millennium; this is the kingdom that is coming. The Stone is Jesus.

Let me read to you out of Matthew's Gospel, chapter 21, verses 42–44:

"*Jesus saith unto them, Did ye never read in the scriptures, The stone which the builders rejected, the same is become the*

head of the corner: this is the Lord's doing, and it is marvel-
lous in our eyes? Therefore say I unto you, The kingdom of God
shall be taken from you, and given to a nation bringing forth
the fruits thereof. And whosoever shall fall on this stone [Jews—
the stone hewn out of a mountain] *shall be broken: but on*
whomsoever it shall fall, it will grind him to powder."

That little Stone, hewn out of a mountain, came rolling down
the mountainside, hit that image and crushed it. Then that little Stone began to become a big stone. It grew and it grew
and it grew until it became a great kingdom that covered all
the earth.

That is Jesus. That is His kingdom. And that is the New World
order. He is the saving Stone. "Neither is there salvation in any
other . . . ."

Not only is He the saving stone, but He is the foundation
Stone: "Upon this rock I will build my church; and the gates
of hell shall not prevail against it."

He is the crushing Stone. The little Stone came out of the
mountain and broke in pieces the iron, the clay, the brass, the
silver, the gold.

Jesus Christ will destroy this Babylonian system. He will tear
down this system that began back in Genesis, chapter 10, with
the Tower of Babel and has been perpetuated ever since in
all governments. Finally it is becoming global in its extent. Jesus
will crush it. He will bring the nations to the winepress of the
wrath of God (Rev. 19:5). He will rule the nations with a rod
of iron in the glorious New World order.

The Confessions of a King

Introduction

It is a marvelous, an amazing thing when rulers of the world recognize who the real Ruler is.

- He is a fool who refuses to acknowledge God—Psalm 14:1.
- Nebuchadnezzar made a confession that every world leader needs to make.
- He made a declaration that rocked his empire and shook the souls of his subjects.

Message

I. OUR GOD IS THE GOD WHO REVEALS HIMSELF TO MANKIND.

> **NOTE:** Three specific ways God reveals Himself:
> 1. Creation—Psalm 19:1–4
> 2. Bible—Hebrews 1:1–3
> 3. Son—Hebrews 1:1–3
>   - John 1:1, 2, 14 and 18
>   - John 14:1–10

II. OUR GOD RULES IN THE AFFAIRS OF MANKIND.

> **NOTE:** Three classic examples of God ruling in the affairs of men and nations
> **Example 1**—Pharaoh of Egypt—Exodus 5:1, 2
> **Example 2**—Nebuchadnezzar of Babylon (text)
> **Example 3**—Cyrus of Persia—Isaiah 44:24–28

- Psalm 75:6, 7—"Promotion...."
- Proverbs 21:1—"The king's heart...."

Reminder: He who rules in the affairs of nations rules in your life and mine.

- God gave you life—Genesis 2:7.
- God sustains your life—Acts 17:28.
- God has the prerogative to govern your life.
  —govern the way you spend your time—Ephesians 5.16.
  —govern the way you spend your money—Malachi 3:10.
  —govern the way you spend your energy—Luke 9:23–25.

III. OUR GOD IS THE GOD WHO REDEEMS THE FALLEN OF MANKIND.

NOTE: Story of salvation: greatest story ever told

It is:

1. A story of love—John 3:16.
2. A story of blood—Hebrews 9:12.
3. A story of faith—Ephesians 2:8, 9.
4. A story that needs to be told again and again.
   - "Tell me the story of Jesus...."
   - "Tell it again."
   - Tell it as it is to men as they are.
   - Tell them Jesus died.
   - Tell them Jesus was buried.
   - Tell them Jesus arose.
   - Tell them Jesus is coming again.

CHAPTER FIVE

The Confessions of a King

46. *Then the king Nebuchadnezzar fell upon his face, and worshipped Daniel, and commanded that they should offer an oblation and sweet odours unto him.*

47. *The king answered unto Daniel, and said, Of a truth it is, that your God is a God of gods, and a Lord of kings, and a revealer of secrets, seeing thou couldest reveal this secret.*

48. *Then the king made Daniel a great man, and gave him many great gifts, and made him ruler over the whole province of Babylon, and chief of the governors over all the wise men of Babylon.*

49. *Then Daniel requested of the king, and he set Shadrach, Meshach, and Abednego, over the affairs of the province of Babylon: but Daniel sat in the gate of the king.*—Dan. 2:46–49.

The middle of verse 47 says, "Of a truth it is, that your God is a God of gods." We must reckon with the fact that Nebuchadnezzar was a pagan. He lived in a pagan world, ruled over a pagan kingdom and worshiped pagan gods. He is called the Excellency, the Lord of lords, a great king, the greatest of his era. He built the Hanging Gardens of Babylon, one of the world's seven wonders. He conquered the world. What he says to Daniel, "Your God is the God of all gods," is a tremendous statement. It is a miraculous thing when rulers of the world acknowledge who the true Ruler is.

There is but one king—King Jesus, the Lord of lords, the King of kings, the Commandant of commandants, the Commander in Chief. Nobody can take His place.

Is He Lord of your life? I didn't ask, "Is He your Saviour?" I believe every person here tonight is saved. I have but one single burden, and that is that you come to know Jesus Christ as your Saviour. But He needs to be more than your Saviour; He needs to be your Lord.

You and I are living under the Lordship of Jesus Christ. That means that everything we say, everything we think, every dime we spend, every place we go, every thought we conceive, every step we take, is under His authority. He is in charge. He is the Master; we are the servants.

It is a marvelous thing for a king like Nebuchadnezzar to acknowledge that the real God is the God of Daniel. He is a fool who refuses to acknowledge God. "The fool hath said in his heart, There is no God" (Ps. 14:1).

Nebuchadnezzar made a confession that day that every world leader needs to make. One thing that would change the complexion of our military forces, our economic system and our governmental system would be if men would recognize who God is. And it's about time that Christians recognized it also. He is the Great God of the universe.

(Some things disturb me. One is when somebody refers to God as "the man upstairs"; the other is when a young man refers to his daddy as "the old man." So don't ever say either in my presence.)

Nebuchadnezzar made a declaration that rocked his empire and shocked the souls of all his subjects. When the king spoke, everybody listened. This wasn't done in a corner. There were

120 provinces from India to Ethiopia, and every subject in Nebuchadnezzar's kingdom heard sooner or later that this man had acknowledged who God really is.

Look again at verse 47: "The king answered unto Daniel, and said, Of a truth it is, that your God is a God of gods." Now understand, this man was a pagan, raised in a pagan environment. That's coming a long way for one like Nebuchadnezzar to come out all of a sudden and say, "Your God is a God of gods."

He is the God of Abraham. He is the God of Isaac. He is the God of Jacob. He is the God and Father of our Lord Jesus Christ. He is the God of all creation. He is the God of every covenant in the Bible. He is the God of the consummation of all things. He is the Ancient of days. He is the Alpha, the Omega, the Beginning, the End, the First, the Last, the Start, the Finish. He is the God of all grace and mercy, peace, comfort, kindness, compassion, love, life, light, liberty, power and majesty, dominion and greatness, goodness and gentleness. He is the God of judgment. He is the God of justice. He is the God of eternity! There is no end to His reign.

There are three things about this God that Nebuchadnezzar acknowledged as the God of all gods and the King of all lords.

I. A GOD WHO REVEALS HIMSELF

God is not a silent God. He has always made Himself known. In these three ways God reveals Himself.

First, God reveals Himself in the *creation.* How can anybody behold the stars, the moon, the sun, the planets, the trees, the birds, the flowers, the grass, the creeks, the rivers, the streams, the oceans, the raindrop, the snowflake and say, "There is no God," and say all of this came into being accidentally? Or that there has been this long period of evolution. I heard Dr. M. F. Ham say a long time ago, "You fellows who believe that [evolution], ought to hitch yourself up to a jackass, but first apologize to the jackass."

God is a God of creation.

Turn to Psalm 19. This is inerrant, infallible, pure, perfect, powerful, productive. There is nothing like it in all the world.

"The heavens declare the glory of God; and the firmament sheweth his handywork. Day unto day uttereth speech, and night unto night sheweth knowledge. There is no speech nor language, where their voice is not heard. Their line is gone out through all the earth, and their words to the end of the world. In them hath he set a tabernacle for the sun."—Vss. 1-4.

Look at the stars, the moon, the planets: look at creation. God is the perfect designer behind them all. He has revealed Himself in creation.

Second, He has revealed Himself in the *written Word.* This Bible is infallible, inspired, inerrant. Hebrews 1:1: "God, who at sundry times and in divers manners spake in time past unto the fathers by the prophets...."

God spoke and holy men of God wrote as they were moved, or carried along, by the Holy Spirit. This Word did not just happen. This Word is not a compilation of somebody's dream or concocted idea of what ought to be. This is the Word of God, and God has spoken to us "in time past unto the fathers by the prophets." Men wrote as they were inspired of the Holy Spirit.

God spoke in creation, in the written revelation, and third, through His Son. Continue reading in Hebrews: "God, who at sundry times and in divers manners spake in time past unto the fathers by the prophets, Hath in these last days spoken unto us by his Son...." God revealed Himself by His Son.

Turn to John's Gospel, chapter 1. Look at verses 1, 2, 14 and 18. John's Gospel is called the eagle Gospel because it soars beyond the synoptics. It has more theology, more Father-Son relationships than do Matthew, Mark or Luke. John, in one stroke of the pen, takes us out of the realm of the earthly into the realm of the heavenly. He takes us away from time into eternity, away from mundane things of earth to splendorous things of Heaven.

Verse 1: "In the beginning was the Word, and the Word was with God, and the Word was God. The same was in the beginning with God."

Verse 14: "And the Word was made flesh, and dwelt among us, (and we beheld his glory, the glory as of the only begotten of the Father,) full of grace and truth."

Verse 18: "No man hath seen God at any time; the only begotten Son . . . he hath declared him."

The angel said to Mary, 'The Holy Ghost shall overshadow thee, and that holy thing which shall be born of thee shall be called the Son of the Highest.' Jesus Christ, the eternal Word, became flesh and dwelt among us as the only fathered Son, the only begotten Son, the only one whom He begat. The only begotten Son, which is in the bosom of the Father, He hath declared Him, revealed Him, unveiled Him, shown Him to us.

I'm speaking now about how God has revealed Himself; first, in creation; second, in the Scriptures; third, in the person of His dear Son.

Jesus said in John 14:

"Let not your heart be troubled: ye believe in God, believe also in me. In my Father's house are many mansions."

I don't like that song, "Lord, build me a cabin in the corner of Gloryland." I don't want a cabin in a corner; I want a mansion on a hilltop in Glory. "In my Father's house are many mansions."

As a youngster, I was about the smallest fellow in my neighborhood. There are always some big bullies around. When they would start on me, I didn't run off to my neighbor's house—I went to my father's house. When I got hungry, I didn't go to my neighbor's house—I went to my father's house. When I got cold or got scared of the dark or when things weren't going so well, I didn't go running off to my neighbor's house—I went to my father's house. Why? Because in my father's house was warmth, shelter, food, love, companionship, understanding, patience, kindness, goodness, mercy—everything a lad needed.

But I know a story much better! The big, big bully—the Devil—is out to get us, out to destroy us. But we can find refuge in our Father's house.

"In my Father's house are many mansions: if it were not so, I would have told you. I go to prepare a place for you. And if I go and prepare a place for you, I will come again, and receive you unto myself; that where I am, there ye may be also. And whither I go ye know, and the way ye know. Thomas saith unto him, Lord, we know not whither thou goest; and how can we know the way? Jesus saith unto him, I am the way, the truth, and the life: no man cometh unto the Father, but by me. If ye had known me, ye should have known my Father also: and from henceforth ye know him, and have seen him. Philip saith unto him, Lord, shew us the Father, and it sufficeth us. Jesus saith unto him, Have I been so long time with you, and yet hast thou not known me, Philip? He that hath seen me hath seen the Father; and how sayest thou then, Shew us the Father? Believest thou not that I am in the Father, and the Father in me? the words that I speak unto you I speak not of myself: but the Father that dwelleth in me, he doeth the works."—Vss. 2–10.

God, the God whom Nebuchadnezzar recognized, Daniel's God, your God, my God, the God of the universe, is the God who reveals Himself in *Creation*, in *Scripture*, and by *His Son.*

II. A GOD WHO RULES

Our God is the God who rules in the affairs of mankind. There are three classic examples of God ruling in the affairs of men and nations.

Example one: *Pharaoh of Egypt.* Under the authority of God, Moses went down to Pharaoh's house one day and said to him, 'Let My people go that they can worship Me, that they may sacrifice to Me, adore Me, honor Me, that they can claim Me as the God of Israel.' God said, "Let my people go." Pharaoh answered, "Who is God that I should obey?"

Don't ever ask that question, "Who is God that I should obey His voice?" God is full of answers. He gave Pharaoh ten answers, ten plagues, including the death of the firstborn. And after it was over, Pharaoh didn't have to ask, "Who is God?" Now He knew who God was. And when God finishes with you and me, we too will know who He is.

God rules in the affairs of all mankind, all nations and all men.

The second classic example is in my text: *Nebuchadnezzar of Babylon.* I have already extolled that point. I've said that Nebuchadnezzar was a pagan, but God loves pagans, too. And He can save pagans, too. God wants to reach out to all men through us.

What if Daniel had fallen down on the job? What if he had said, "I'm seven or eight hundred miles from home. Nobody will ever know it. So I'll drink the king's wine. I'll eat the king's food. I'll fall right in with the crowd of the world"? But the Bible says Daniel said, "N-O!"

Young people, you had better learn to say *no*—maybe the hardest word in the English language to say. But tomorrow you'll be glad that you stood for right.

Let me say again: the reason Daniel could handle the lions at ninety is that he learned how to handle temptation at *nineteen.* Learn to say *no.* Be a real soldier for God.

Stand up, stand up for Jesus,
Ye soldiers of the cross;

**Lift high His royal banner;
It must not suffer loss.**

It happened right here in Dallas many years ago. Some smart aleck, who thought he could downgrade God, downgrade Christianity and downgrade all of the Christian faith, rented a large hall and went on a tirade against Christ and Christianity. In a packed auditorium he went from A to Z, ran the gamut of all the things he could think of to say against God and against Christ.

When he had finished, in a moment of silence, two little girls, way back in the back stood up and started singing, "Stand up, stand up for Jesus, ye soldiers of the cross." Before they got through the first stanza, people began to stand all over that great audience. By the time they got to the last stanza, every person was on his feet singing, "Stand up, stand up for Jesus, ye soldiers of the cross."

Young people, stand up for Jesus. Stand up for what is right. When you are old and feeble, you'll be so glad you did. You'll still have a brain if you say no to drugs. Say yes to alcohol, and your brain will soon be gone. Don't do it. Say *no* to those things that are sure to ruin you. Nebuchadnezzar observed Daniel and said to Daniel, "Your God is *the* God."

God reveals Himself; God rules in the affairs of men and nations.

The third classic example is Cyrus of Persia. In Isaiah 44:24–27, God called a pagan by the name of Cyrus by his name almost 200 years before he was born.

"Thus saith the Lord, thy redeemer, and he that formed thee from the womb, I am the Lord that maketh all things; that stretcheth forth the heavens alone; that spreadeth abroad the earth by myself; That frustrateth the tokens of the liars, and maketh diviners mad; that turneth wise men backward, and maketh their knowledge foolish; That confirmeth the word of

his servant, and performeth the counsel of his messengers; That saith to Jerusalem, Thou shalt be inhabited; and to the cities of Judah, Ye shall be built, and I will raise up the decayed places thereof: That saith to the deep, Be dry, and I will dry up thy rivers."

God didn't only dry up the Jordan River and the Red Sea, but He dried up the Euphrates River. And they went across dry shod. Listen to verse 28:

"That saith of Cyrus, He is my shepherd, and shall perform all my pleasure: even saying to Jerusalem, Thou shalt be built; and to the temple, Thy foundation shall be laid."

Remember now that Jerusalem and the Temple had been destroyed, but God is looking ahead. And in the days that Cyrus ruled, beginning at 536 B. C., he issued a decree that all captives in Babylon who wanted to, could go back to Jerusalem and rebuild the city and the Temple. That was in the sixth century before Christ. In the year 444 B. C., a hundred years later, Artaxerxes was king over Persia.

One day Nehemiah, his cupbearer, went in before the king, put down the cup; and the king said to him, 'What's the matter with you, Nehemiah? There's something wrong. I can tell by your countenance.'

Nehemiah replied, 'I just got word from Jerusalem that all the walls and all the gates are torn down, and the whole city lies in the ruin.'

Artaxerxes asked, 'What can I do?'

Nehemiah, praying to God for wisdom to know what to say, replied, 'If you would, just let me go back and view the remains of my city and start rebuilding.'

The end of that story is this: Artaxerxes went back into the archives of the Medo-Persian empire and found a letter, the decree that Cyrus had written almost a hundred years before, to free God's people and let them go back to Jerusalem.

They went back, built the city and the Temple.

God rules in the affairs of men and nations. I remind you of Psalm 75:6, 7, "For promotion cometh neither from the east, nor from the west, nor from the south. But God is the judge: he putteth down one, and setteth up another." And of Proverbs 21:1, "The king's heart is in the hand of the Lord, as the rivers of water: he turneth it whithersoever he will."

Our President is in God's hands. Yeltsin is in God's hand. This bearded rebel down here in Cuba, Castro, is in God's hand. God is letting them have their day. But one day He will step in and rule the world. And there will be no more iron curtains, no more Berlin Walls, no more anti-God movements. Jesus Christ, the King of kings, will ultimately rule in the heart and life of every nation and every man.

"Let this mind be in you, which was also in Christ Jesus: Who, being in the form of God, thought it not robbery to be equal with God: But made himself of no reputation, and took upon him the form of a servant, and was made in the likeness of men: And being found in fashion as a man, he humbled himself, and became obedient unto death, even the death of the cross. Wherefore God also hath highly exalted him, and given him a name which is above every name: That at the name of Jesus every knee should bow, of things in heaven, and things in earth, and things under the earth; and that every tongue should confess that Jesus Christ is Lord, to the glory of God the Father."— Phil. 2:5–11.

Every God-hater, every Christ-rejecter, every church-hater, every God-denier will one day bow before Jesus Christ and exclaim, "He is the Lord!"

I ought to tell you that He who rules in the affairs of nations, rules in your life and mine. God gave us life: "And the Lord God formed man of the dust of the ground, and breathed into his nostrils the breath of life; and man became a living soul."

Where are the evolutionists? Listen to me! Nobody has ever proven God's Word to be wrong. The burden of proof is on that agnostic, atheistic, unbelieving crowd out there who say there is no God. I'm not going to try to prove there is a God. God said it, it is written, it is revealed, and that's good enough for me.

When Moses went to the University of Egypt, those teachers had some wild, weird stories about how creation came in. One said this: "Once upon a time there was this huge cosmic egg just floating around in space. One day when the temperature reached the right degree, this egg cracked open, and out hatched creation." Isn't that great!

Moses: "Teacher, please, can I ask a question?"

"Yes sir, Mr. Moses."

"Where did the egg come from?"

That was the end of that story.

So when Moses sat down to write the book of Genesis, he didn't write, "In the beginning there was a huge cosmic egg," but, "In the beginning God created the heaven and the earth."

God made you and me in His own likeness. He gave us breath. So He has every right to govern each life because He sustains it. Paul said in his great sermon on Mars' Hill, "And in him we live and move and have our being."

God has the prerogative to govern each life in every area. God has the right to govern how we spend our time. Paul said, "Redeeming the time, because the days are evil." God has every right to govern the way we spend our money. 'Bring ye all the tithes into the storehouse, that there be no gatherings when I come.' God has every right to tell us how to spend our energy, our lives. Jesus put it this way in Luke 9:23–25:

"If any man will come after me, let him deny himself, and take up his cross daily, and follow me. For whosoever will save

his life shall lose it: but whosoever will lose his life for my sake,
the same shall save it. For what is a man advantaged, if he
gain the whole world, and lose himself, or be cast away?"

So many Christians are too busy trying to save their own
lives with another dollar, with another ounce of energy to make
another dime, another dollar, another profit, to make an
impression on somebody, to climb a little bit higher on the
corporate ladder.

"For whosoever will save his life shall lose it; but whosoever
shall lose his life for my sake and the gospel's, the same shall
save it. . . . Whosoever therefore shall be ashamed of me and
of my words in this adulterous and sinful generation; of him
also shall the Son of man be ashamed, when he cometh in the
glory of his Father with the holy angels."—Mark 8:35–38.

Talking to His followers, Jesus said, 'Lose your life for My
sake, and you will save it. Save it for your sake, and you will
lose it.'

God has the prerogative to govern your life and mine.

III. A GOD WHO REDEEMS

God redeems all the fallen of mankind. The story of salvation is the greatest story ever told. It is a story of love—"For
God so loved the world, that he gave his only begotten Son,
that whosoever. . ." is preordained? No. That whosoever is
elected? No. That whosoever is rich? No. That whosoever is
wise? No. That whosoever is educated? No. That whosoever
is sophisticated? No. ". . .that whosoever believeth in him
should not perish, but have everlasting life."

It's a *love* story—"God so loved. . . ." It's a story of *blood*—
"Neither by the blood of goats and calves, but by his own blood
he entered in once into the holy place, having obtained eternal redemption for us" (Heb. 9:12). It is the story of *faith*—
"For by grace are ye saved through faith; and that not of

your selves: it is the gift of God: Not of works, lest any man should boast" (Eph. 2:8, 9).

This story needs to be told over and over again. Oh, for a thousand tongues! If I could have the ear of every nationality, of every tongue on the earth, and could speak all the languages of the world, I would say with the early church father, *"If the highest heavens were my pulpit, and all the earth my parish, Jesus alone would be my text."* This story deserves to be told.

> **Tell me the story of Jesus,**
> **Write on my heart every word;**
> **Tell me the story most precious,**
> **Sweetest that ever was heard.**

This story needs to be told again and again to men as they are, just like it is. Tell them Jesus died. Tell them Jesus was buried. Tell them Jesus arose. Tell them Jesus is at the right hand of God to make intercession for them. Tell them Jesus went away but not to stay, that He is coming back again. And ask if they are ready.

An Image of Gold

Introduction

Satan has always had his representatives: diabolical, destructive, deadly.

- His ambassadors are too many to count.
- His emissaries are never idle.
- His cohorts are dedicated to him; they serve him with diligence, dedication, determination.
  —The Devil is religious.
  —The Devil comes to church.

  (I think I ought to tell you again that he has to ride with somebody.)
- The Devil uses people to propagate false doctrine.
- He uses people to execute his will.
- He uses people to offer counterfeit religion.
- He uses people to deceive the multitudes.
- He uses people in **high** and **low** places.
- He uses the **big** and the **little**.
- He uses the **young** and the **old**.
- He uses the **fat** and the **skinny**.
- He uses the **rich** and the **poor**.
- He uses the **educated** and the **uneducated**.
- He uses the **lost** and the **saved**.

Tragedy: Sometimes he uses **good** people to do **bad** things.

Warning: Ephesians 4:27—*"Neither give place to the devil."*
(Give Satan an inch, and he will take a mile.)

NOTE: It appears from chapter 2 that Nebuchadnezzar
was on the right track and moving in the right
direction ("confession"—2:47).
(The Devil will sidetrack you when he can; get you
involved in a **good** thing to the neglect of the **best**
thing.)

QUESTION: What **good** thing did you allow to take you from
your responsibility? soul winning? visitation? etc.

- Was making a dollar more important than making a visit?
- Was a sandwich more important than a soul?
- Was a picnic more important than a prayer meeting?
- Was catering to boss more important than pleasing the Lord?
- Was a social contact more important than spiritual contact?
- Was a business deal more important than Bible study?

NOTE: Nebuchadnezzar soon forgot his confession.
  - He soon forgot his concern.
  - He soon forgot his commitment.
  - He soon forgot his promise.
NOTE: How soon we forget the "yesterdays of our Christian experience."
  - Yesterday, God was your Source of strength.
  - Yesterday, the Bible was your number one Book.
  - Yesterday, Jesus was your Hero.
  - Yesterday, your Sunday school class was your life.
  - Yesterday, your place in choir was your "crown of rejoicing."
  - Yesterday, souls were your concern.
  - Yesterday, tithing was your first payment and

greatest investment. (What did you spend it for?)
- Yesterday, prayer was your priority.
- Yesterday, prayer meeting was a "must."
- Yesterday, you lived to serve God and to go to church.
- Yesterday, you cultivated Christian friendships.

But: What about today? now? tomorrow?
- Who is first in your life?
- What is occupying your time?
- Where are your priorities?
- What is your relationship to God, the Bible, the church, your pastor?

NOTE: The story in my text is an amazing story. It is the story of three young men whose faith and courage have inspired generations of Christians to stay true to God.
- They were young men.
- They were bold young men.
- They were courageous young men.
- They were committed young men.
- They were consecrated young men.

   —They defied a king.
   —They demonstrated their faith.
   —They displayed their character.
   —They declared their intentions.
   —They discovered the power of God.

(They would not bow nor bend nor burn.)

Message

I. IMAGE OF GOLD WAS AN ATTEMPT TO UNIFY IDOL WORSHIP.

NOTE: The cry among religionists today is: "Let's get together."
- God says "No!"
- God says, *"Come out from among them. . . ."*
- God says, *"I am a jealous God. . . ."*

NOTE: Cardinal sin among God's people: idolatry.
- Christians today worship pleasure—II Timothy 3:1–5.
- Christians today bow at altar of materialism.
- Christians today elevate self—egotism.

NOTE: Self dies hard.
- Luke 9:23
- Galatians 2:20

NOTE: Anything/anybody that takes affection, devotion, dedication that God should get from us is an idol:
- Exodus 20:3—*"Thou shalt have no other. . . ."*
- Isaiah 45:18–23
- Isaiah 46:9, 10
- I Thessalonians 1:9—*"Turned to God from idols. . . ."*

II. IMAGE OF GOLD REMINDS US THAT ALL ATTEMPTS TO DETHRONE GOD WILL FAIL.

NOTE: This image represents the finest Babylon could offer.

It represents the god of this world system.
- 90 feet tall
- 9 feet wide
- Pure gold

NOTE: This Book tells us about the only true God.

I am representing the true and living God.
- Not 90 feet tall
- Not 9 feet wide
- Not pure gold

But: I am one of God's representatives on Earth. (Pope—"Vicar of Christ")

NOTE: Paul—II Corinthians 5:20—*"Now then we are ambassadors...."*

NOTE: Attempts to dethrone God:
- Devil himself tried—Isaiah 14:12–15.
- Liberal theologians—mid-sixties: "God Is Dead"
- Humanists: New Age Movement "Humanist Manifesto"
- Every person who puts anything in God's place attempts to dethrone Him.
- Antichrist—II Thessalonians 2

Illustration: Man who challenged God to strike him with lightning.
(God was busy, so He sent a gnat that got into his throat and choked him to death.)

III. IMAGE OF GOLD BROUGHT OUT VERY BEST IN GOD'S PEOPLE.

King's threat—verse 6
Babylonians' accusation—verses 8–12

NOTE: Observe three things about Daniel's companions:
1. They were **victimized**—verse 12.
2. They were **venturesome**—verses 14–18.
   Note: Verse 18—"If not...."
3. They were **victorious**—verses 23–25.
   - "Fourth man theme"—fourth Man: Jesus
   - "If Jesus goes with me...."

Conclusion: You, Too...

. . . victimized by Devil
. . . venturesome—"step out by faith"
. . . victorious—Philippians 4:13

Appeal: Take your place among heroes of the Faith.

CHAPTER SIX

An Image of Gold

1. *Nebuchadnezzar the king made an image of gold, whose height was threescore cubits, and the breadth thereof six cubits: he set it up in the plain of Dura, in the province of Babylon.*

2. *Then Nebuchadnezzar the king sent to gather together the princes, the governors, and the captains, the judges, the treasurers, the counsellors, the sheriffs, and all the rulers of the provinces, to come to the dedication of the image which Nebuchadnezzar the king had set up.*

3. *Then the princes, the governors, and the captains, the judges, the treasurers, the counsellors, the sheriffs, and all the rulers of the provinces, were gathered together unto the dedication of the image that Nebuchadnezzar the king had set up; and they stood before the image that Nebuchadnezzar had set up.*

4. *Then an herald cried aloud, To you it is commanded, O people, nations, and languages,*

5. *That at what time ye hear the sound of the cornet, flute, harp, sackbut, psaltery, dulcimer, and all kinds of music, ye fall down and worship the golden image that Nebuchadnezzar the king hath set up:*

6. *And whoso falleth not down and worshippeth shall the*

same hour be cast into the midst of a burning fiery furnace.

7. *Therefore at that time, when all the people heard the sound of the cornet, flute, harp, sackbut, psaltery, and all kinds of music, all the people, the nations, and the languages, fell down and worshipped the golden image that Nebuchadnezzar the king had set up.*—Dan. 3:1–7.

Satan is alive and well. Satan has always had his representatives on earth; they are diabolical, destructive, deceptive and deadly. Satan's ambassadors are too many to count. His emissaries have never been idle. His cohorts serve him with devotion, diligence, dedication and determination. The Devil is very religious. He comes to church. In fact, he is more regular than some of the more regular absentees. And every time he comes, he has to hitch a ride with somebody.

The Devil uses people to propagate false doctrine. He uses people to execute his own will, his own plan and his own program. The Devil has drawn the blueprint and has all kinds of imps and personalities to carry through with what he started in the Garden of Eden.

The Devil, being the greatest counterfeiter, uses people to offer a counterfeit religion. He uses people to deceive the multitudes. The Devil uses people in high and low places. He uses big and small people, young and old people, fat and skinny people. He uses the tall and the short, the bright ones and the dull ones. He uses both the rich and poor, those educated and those uneducated. He uses both the lost and the saved.

Can a saved person be demon-possessed? I know Christians can be demon- and Devil-influenced. The tragedy is that sometimes Satan uses *good* people to do *bad* things. Think about that. Satan is so sly, so wise, so conniving, so subtle, so undermining and so deceptive that he uses good people to do his bidding when they do bad things.

Listen to the warning in Ephesians 4:27, where Paul says, "Neither give place to the devil." If you give the Devil an inch, he will take a mile. Nobody ever lost the joy of his religion nor backslid in a blowout. I've heard preachers preach about the Devil and about people. (I've preached on that a few times myself.) I've never known one person to get up on Monday morning or Wednesday morning or Saturday morning and say, "I'm just going to the Devil. I'm giving up God, the church, the Bible—throwing it all to the winds. I'm turning my life over to Satan." But I've seen a lot of people allow the Devil to get a toehold, then a foothold, then a stronghold; then it was all over.

It starts when people begin to neglect their Christian duties and responsibilities. One of the most effective weapons Satan has is discouragement, because he knows God can't use a discouraged Christian. He wants to get you to neglect your duties.

He never comes with some big, outrageous, unthinkable sin for you to commit. Oh, no! He doesn't work that way. Do you think the Devil would come to a man who has been sober for fifty years and say, "Come on. I want you to take a drink"? Not on your life. But he will say, "Well, it's not really important that you go to church next Sunday or that you go out visiting this week or that you tithe this week." That is how the Devil works.

This wise, conniving, scheming, subtle, suggestive Devil just comes at you in a nice way: "Well, now, after all, since you work hard all week, you need Sunday for your own."

"Well, say that again, Devil; that sounds pretty good." And you listen a second time.

Or the Devil says, "Now you know you've got to lay aside for a rainy day. So don't give too much money to the church."

"Say that again, Devil. Tell me about my family responsibilities. I want to do the best for them."

Wait a minute! First things first. "Seek ye first the kingdom of God, and his righteousness; and all these things shall be added unto you."

I'm saying, the Devil will say, "Now it won't hurt you to make some friendships with others outside the church. After all, so what? You work with them every day. So why not run with them, associate with them, be with them?"

Then is when you'll start drifting away from God, the church and your circle of Christian friends. It happens so subtly that many don't recognize how the Devil works. Don't let it happen!

It appears from chapter 2 that Nebuchadnezzar was on the right track and moving in the right direction. Chapter 2, verse 47: "The king answered unto Daniel, and said, Of a truth it is, that your God is a God of gods." But in chapter 3 he has built his own god. The Devil sidetracked Nebuchadnezzar. And he will sidetrack you every chance he gets. He will get you to thinking everything under the sun is more important than going to church, serving God, winning souls, reading your Bible, praying and giving. He'll make everything seem bigger and better than going to church. After all, going to church is not the easiest thing in the world to do. The Devil makes it as hard as he can.

Listen! If church-attending is a burden instead of a blessing, then you have a spiritual problem. If it is a job instead of a joy, you have a spiritual problem. If it is a drag instead of a desire, you have a spiritual problem. It is time for you to get on your face before God and ask Him to help you enjoy your religion.

Christians ought to have as good a time going to Heaven as the Devil's crowd has in going to Hell. I'd rather subdue a fanatic any day than raise a corpse. I don't care if you shout, as long as you walk straight when you hit ground.

The Devil will sidetrack you. He will get you involved in a good thing to the exclusion of the best thing. And priority number one is winning souls and being faithful to God and to your church.

Let me ask you, What good thing did you allow to take you from your responsibility this last week? What good thing kept you from soul winning this past week? What good thing kept you from visitation this past week? What good thing kept you from doing what you were supposed to do as a unit head, as a secretary, as a group leader, as a member of the church?

Was making a dollar more important than making a visit? Was a sandwich more important than pleasing the Lord? Was a social contact more important than a spiritual contract? Was a business deal more important than Bible study?

Nebuchadnezzar soon forgot the confession in 2:47, soon forgot his concern, his commitment, his promise: 'God, the God of Daniel, is the God. There is no other. He is the God of all gods.'

How soon we forget the yesterdays of our Christian experience. Yesterday God was your Source of strength. You depended on Him completely—yesterday. Yesterday the Bible was your number one Book. You just couldn't wait to read it—yesterday. Yesterday Jesus was your Hero; today someone out there on your job or in your community, has become your hero. Jesus now has taken second place. You lived to work and labor and share and teach your Sunday school class—yesterday. Yesterday your place in the choir was your crown of rejoicing. You loved to sing the songs of Zion, tell the old, old story— yesterday.

Yesterday souls were your chief concern. You just couldn't wait to tell somebody what God had done for you and what He could do for him. You just couldn't wait to get out and ask, "Where can I go? Give me names to visit, somebody to win to Jesus"—yesterday. Yesterday tithing was your first payment, your greatest investment out of your paycheck. On what good thing did you spend your tithe this week?

Yesterday prayer was your priority. What a joy to get down on your knees before God and say, "Dear God, I don't have much to offer, but here am I. Send me where You want me to go.

Let me do what You want me to do." Just getting down on your knees and talking to God was your priority—yesterday.

Yesterday you lived to serve God and go to church. Yesterday prayer meeting was a must in your life. You couldn't wait for Sunday: it was a must.

Yesterday you cultivated Christian friendships and fellowships. But what about today? What about now? What about tomorrow? Who is first now? What is occupying your time? Taking your thought processes? What are you giving yourself to? Another dime, another dollar, another raise, another rung on the ladder? What are your priorities?

This generation ought to get ready for Christ's coming because this generation may witness His return. When we get His coming in the proper prospective, another dime, another dollar will not mean anything to us.

I'm talking to some who yesterday could not care less about material things; now you are involved in them today. Where is the prospect of the coming of Christ? What is your relationship to God, the Bible, church, your fellow Christians, your pastor?

The story in my text is that of three young men whose faith and courage have inspired generations of Christians to stay true to God. Young people, let this example of these young men be your example. Let them be your heroes, the ones you look up to, the ones you take a lesson from. Don't make your heroes some half-witted musicians. Don't cry when they have fights at these rock concerts. Let them tear up the instruments and their meeting places. I don't want anybody to get hurt, but I don't mind if their instruments are destroyed. That crowd is not fit to walk on the streets to influence innocent young people and poison their minds. Let's declare a spiritual war against them. I need help: some generals in the army, some lieutenants, sergeants, privates, some foot soldiers. I can't do it alone.

We need to declare war on the evils in our society. These

three young men were bold and brave, daring and courageous. They were committed. They defied a king, demonstrated their faith, displayed their character, declared their intentions and discovered the power of God. I like to think of them as the three who would not bow nor bend nor burn.

That is in introduction.

I. ATTEMPT TO UNIFY IDOL WORSHIP

The image of gold was an attempt to unify idol worship.

The cry among the religionists today is "Let's all get together. It doesn't matter what we believe." But it does matter. I do not want to be associated with anybody who denies the inspiration of the Scripture, the virgin birth and the resurrection. You will not find God where the pulpit is occupied by one who denies the virgin birth of Jesus, the inspiration of the Scripture, and the resurrection of our Lord.

Hear me! God doesn't say, "Get together," but "Get apart." "Come out from among them, and be ye separate, saith the Lord."

God says, "I am a jealous God." The cardinal sin among God's people in every age is idolatry. Christians today are worshiping the idol god of pleasure. Read it in II Timothy 3:1–5. There it says, "Men shall be lovers of pleasure more than lovers of God."

Christians today are bowing down at the altar of materialism. Christians are elevating self. They have developed a bad case of egotism. Self dies hard. In Luke 9:23 Jesus said, "If any man will come after me, let him deny himself." We read in Galatians 2:20, "I am crucified with Christ: nevertheless I live; yet not I, but Christ liveth in me."

Anything that takes the affection, the devotion, the dedication, the love that you should give to God, becomes an idol. Exodus 20 says, "Thou shalt have no other gods before me."

Isaiah, chapter 45:18 says:

"For thus saith the Lord that created the heavens; God him- self that formed the earth and made it; he hath established it, he created it not in vain, he formed it to be inhabited: I am the Lord; and there is none else."

You say, "But aren't all these other religions right?" No. They are dead wrong, or we are wrong. If Christianity isn't the only way and Christ isn't the only way, we might as well throw out the Bible. You say, "I've got some Mormon friends, some Budd- hist friends." Then pray that they will get saved. "I am the Lord; and there is none else."

"I have not spoken in secret, in a dark place of the earth: I said not unto the seed of Jacob, Seek ye me in vain: I the Lord speak righteousness, I declare things that are right. Assemble yourselves and come; draw near together, ye that are escaped of the nations: they have no knowledge that set up the wood of their graven image, and pray unto a god that cannot save."—Vss. 19, 20.

God says that about false religions. They don't know what they're doing; they have no knowledge. He said,

"Tell ye, and bring them near; yea, let them take counsel together: who hath declared this from ancient time? who hath told it from that time? have not I the Lord? and there is no God else beside me; a just God and a Saviour; there is none beside me. Look unto me, and be ye saved, all the ends of the earth: for I am God, and there is none else. I have sworn by myself, the word is gone out of my mouth in righteousness, and shall not return, That unto me every knee shall bow, every tongue shall swear."—Vss. 21–23.

"Remember the former things of old: for I am God, and there is none else; I am God, and there is none like me, Declaring the end from the beginning, and from ancient times the things that are not yet done, saying, My counsel shall stand, and I will do all my pleasure."—Isa. 46:9, 10.

There is no other God, only the God of Abraham, Isaac, Jacob, and the God of this Book. First Thessalonians 1:9 declares, "...how ye turned to God from idols to serve the living and true God."

I say, the image of gold was an attempt to get all people together and worship an idol, a pagan god—unification, ecumenism—whatever you want to call it. But God says in II Corinthians 6, "Wherefore come out from among them, and be ye separate...and touch not the unclean thing; and I will receive you, And will be a Father unto you, and ye shall be my sons and daughters...."

II. ATTEMPTS TO DETHRONE GOD

The image of gold reminds us that all the attempts to dethrone God will fail. Anytime man sets up an idol god, he is attempting to dethrone the God of Abraham, Isaac and Jacob, the God of the Bible, the God and Father of our Lord Jesus Christ.

This image represents the very finest that Babylon could offer. It represents the gold of this world system. Ninety feet tall, nine feet broad, of pure gold.

This Book tells us about the only true God. I am here as God's representative. I'm not ninety feet tall nor nine feet wide; I'm not of pure gold, but I'm God's ambassador, God's spokesman in this pulpit, God's representative to you.

Somebody says, "The pope is the vicar of Christ." He is no more the vicar of Christ than I am. I have just as much authority as he. God has not picked out one guru on earth and said, "This is the only representative." Paul says in II Corinthians 5:20, "Now then we are ambassadors for Christ, as though God did beseech you by us: we pray you in Christ's stead, be ye reconciled to God."

Who is speaking for God? The man with the Book!

There have been many attempts to dethrone God. The Devil

himself tried it according to Isaiah 14:13, 14: "I will exalt my throne above the stars of God: I will sit also upon the mount of the congregation, in the sides of the north: I will ascend above the heights of the clouds; I will be like the most High."

Anytime one starts thinking about being bigger, better, richer and whatever else, he is heading for a downfall. "Pride goeth before destruction, and an haughty spirit before a fall."

The Devil tried to dethrone God. The liberal theologians tried.

In the mid-sixties there came out of universities in the South this idea that "God is dead." The fake concept went through all the religious periodicals, and the media picked it up: "God is dead." One Saturday night God gave me a poem:

God is dead, the theologians say;
But I know He's not, I've talked with Him today.
Dead, never to live again, they claim,
But alive, alive, to save through His Son's dear name.
Alive, alive, let it be said:
God will be living when the theologians are dead.

Theologians can't dethrone God. The New Age Movement, with its humanist manifesto that says there is no God, can't dethrone God.

I ought to remind you again that anytime you put anything between you and God, you are making that a god, and that is an attempt on your part to dethrone Him. And it won't work. The Antichrist will try it. In II Thessalonians 2 we read that he will put up his image in the restored, rebuilt Temple, cause everybody to bow down and worship him and claim that he is God. That is exactly what Nebuchadnezzar did. He forgot the yesterday of his confession, like many Christians have forgotten the yesterday of your commitment.

Don't do anything to attempt to dethrone the God of the universe!

I read about this fellow who said, "Well, if there's a God, I want Him to prove HIMSELF." So he goes out in the open, defies God and says, "If there's a God, if You're a God, if You're up there, then why don't You strike me dead with lightning?" Since God was busy doing something else, He sent a little gnat that got hung in the man's throat and choked him to death.

> **God works in mysterious ways,**
> **His wonders to perform;**
> **He plants His feet upon the shore**
> **And rides upon the storm.**

III. THE BEST IN GOD'S PEOPLE

The image of God brought out the very best in God's people. These men, these Hebrew children, companions of Daniel, received a threat from the king. Look at verse 6: "And whoso falleth not down and worshippeth shall the same hour be cast into the midst of a burning fiery furnace." We read in subsequent verses that the furnace was so hot that the men who threw them in were burned to death. What a threat! The Babylonians came along and accused these young men (vs. 8) and

9. *They spake and said to the king Nebuchadnezzar, O king, live for ever.*

10. *Thou, O king, hast made a decree...* [that every man is supposed to bow down].

11. *And whoso falleth not down and worshippeth, that he should be cast into the midst of a burning fiery furnace.*

12. *There are certain Jews whom thou hast set over the affairs of the province of Babylon, Shadrach, Meshach, and Abednego; these men, O king, have not regarded thee: they serve not thy gods, nor worship the golden image which thou hast set up.*

13. *Then Nebuchadnezzar in his rage and fury commanded to bring Shadrach, Meshach, and Abednego....*

14. *Nebuchadnezzar spake and said unto them, Is it true,*

O Shadrach, Meshach, and Abednego, do not ye serve my gods, nor worship the golden image which I have set up?

15. *Now if ye be ready that at what time. . .* [and he asked a stupid question, from his point of view], *Who is that God that shall deliver you out of my hands?*

Pharaoh asked that question, "Who is God?" And God gave him one, two, three, four, five, six, seven, eight, nine, ten answers. God said, 'You failed the test. I gave you the answers.'

Who is this God?

16. *Shadrach, Meshach, and Abednego, answered and said to the king, O Nebuchadnezzar, we are not careful to answer thee in this matter.*

17. *If it be so* [if you cast us in], *our God whom we serve is able to deliver us from the burning fiery furnace, and he will deliver us out of thine hand, O king.*

18. *But if not, be it known unto thee, O king, that we will not serve thy gods, nor worship the golden image which thou hast set up.*

'If you throw us in, God will deliver us. But if God doesn't see fit to do it, if we burn in that fiery furnace, if that spells eternity for us, we will not serve your gods.' That proved their character.

Young people, let these be your heroes. Pattern your thinking after their thinking, your conduct after their conduct. Say to the world, "It doesn't matter what comes, we're not going after this world's goods, after the world's temptations. We will not bow down at the altar of rock music, alcohol, drugs, sex. We will serve God. And if we get our heads cut off, it will be but a shortcut to Glory."

These three were *victimized.* In verse 12, the king was told, 'They haven't regarded your edict; they haven't done what you told them to do.' Victimized. Well, Nebuchadnezzar thought he had them right there.

They were not victimized; they were *venturesome:* 'If not—
we're going on through with God, no matter the consequence.'

And they were *victorious.*

23. *And these three men, Shadrach, Meshach, and Abednego,
fell down bound into the midst of the burning fiery furnace.*

24. *Then Nebuchadnezzar the king was astonied, and rose
up in haste, and spake, and said unto his counsellors, Did not
we cast three men bound into the midst of the fire? They
answered and said unto the king, True, O king.* [We did put in
three; and we did bind them.]

25. *He answered and said, Lo, I see four men loose, walking
in the midst of the fire, and they have no hurt; and the form
of the fourth is like the Son of God.*

If Jesus goes with us, we can go anywhere—even into a fiery
furnace. He told us, "I will never leave thee, nor forsake thee."

They were victorious. They came out not even smelling like
smoke. Not a hair on their heads was singed. None of their clothing was burned. The only thing burned were the cords that
bound them.

You, too, will be victimized by Satan, but you can be venturesome. You can step out by faith, and you will be victorious: "I
can do all things through Christ which strengtheneth me."

—— *Outline* 3:26–30 ——————

Changing the Laws

Introduction

God is a God of law and order.
God runs a tight ship.
God keeps perfect records.

- He created a universe totally controlled by laws.
- Every member of Adam's race is subject to laws.
- Every creature God made is subject to laws.
- Laws are an inevitable part of our existence.
- Laws are absolutely necessary to our well-being.
- Laws govern, restrict every area of life.

NOTE: There is no escape from moral and spiritual laws that govern us.
- There is no way to circumvent laws of science and chemistry.
- To resist law is to resist the Lawgiver.
- To break the law is to offend the Lawgiver.
  James 2:10—"Whosoever shall keep the whole law, and yet offend in one point, he is guilty of all."

NOTE: We are admonished in Scripture to obey the laws that govern and guide us.
- I Peter 2:13–15
- Romans 13:1–7

—Not all laws are righteous.
—Not all laws are sanctioned by God.
—Not all laws are based on Scripture.

But: The concept of law/order is of God.

It is God who established principle of law and government.

NOTE: Any law contrary to law of God, or that violates a principle of Scripture, should be circumvented by Christians (Acts 5:29).

Message

I. LAWS OF BABYLON

NOTE: Observe three things:
1. They were permanently fixed and final.
   - Nebuchadnezzar was a tyrant.
   - He was ruthless.
   - He was arrogant.
   - He was discompassionate.
     —His word was the law of the land.
     —When he spoke, his subjects listened.
     —What he commanded, they did.
2. They were universally accepted and obeyed.
   - Nations bowed down before his image.
   - People came from far and near to worship him.
   - He was their god.
3. They were sternly enacted and enforced.
   - NOTE: "Fiery Furnace" (Chap. 3).

NOTE: In spite of universality, the severity, permanency of Nebuchadnezzar's laws, they could be changed!
(Indeed, they were changed.)

NOTE: They were changed in favor of a higher LAW, the Law of God.

II. LAWS OF GOD

Laws of God are
1. Eternal
2. Incomparable
3. Impartial
4. Inviolable
5. Inescapable

Laws of God are
1. Ordained in Heaven
2. Superior to man's laws
3. Forever fixed and unchangeable

QUESTION: Why would God change laws of a worldwide empire just to accommodate three young men?

ANSWER: Plain and obvious to a discerning mind
1. God will do whatever is necessary to preserve His integrity.
2. God will do whatever is necessary to promote His work.
3. God will do whatever is necessary to protect His people.

NOTE: God is constantly in tune with happenings in His world (no surprises).

Poem: "This Is My Father's World"

NOTE: God knows all His creatures, all His people, and He calls them all by name (even knows all the stars—Psalm 147:4).

NOTE: God knows:
- Who you are
- Where you live
- Where you work
- Your telephone number
- Your house number
- Your area code number
- Your zip code number

NOTE: God knows: (cont.)
- Your employment number
- Your Social Security number
- Your bank account number
- Your pulse rate
- Your heartbeat
- Your motives
- Your plans
- Your intentions
- What bothers you
- What threatens you
- What concerns you
- Your blood pressure
- Your bank balance
- Your trials and temptations

NOTE: Job 23:10: *"But he knoweth the way that I take; when he hath tried me, I shall come forth as gold."*

NOTE: Verse 28
- God sent His angel.
- God delivered His servants.
- God changed the laws of the land.

NOTE: The same God who delivered Hebrew children from the fiery furnace can deliver you—Acts 10:34.

NOTE: When I was in seminary over 40 years ago, a song was very popular among the student body: "It Is No Secret."

QUESTION: What is your fiery furnace?

NOTE: If God can change the laws of a heathen kingdom, He can change circumstances of your life.

Conclusion

Let's begin to believe God for some miracles.

- Some of you are bound financially.
- Some of you are imprisoned emotionally.
- Some of you are at a standstill spiritually.

Appeal: Come, let God change what seems to be unchangeable!

- Let Him put out fires in your fiery furnace.
- Let Him break down walls that imprison you.
- Let Him perform a miracle of grace in your life.

CHAPTER SEVEN

Changing the Laws

26. *Then Nebuchadnezzar came near to the mouth of the burning fiery furnace, and spake, and said, Shadrach, Meshach, and Abednego, ye servants of the most high God* [Nebuchadnezzar knew with whom he was dealing. They were servants of the most high God. He acknowledges not only God, but he acknowledges the servants of God.], *come forth, and come hither. Then Shadrach, Meshach, and Abednego, came forth of the midst of the fire.*

27. *And the princes, governors, and captains, and the king's counsellors, being gathered together, saw these men, upon whose bodies the fire had no power* [Isn't that amazing! The furnace was heated seven times hotter than it had ever been heated, and yet the fire had no power on the bodies of these three young men.], *nor was an hair of their head singed, neither were their coats changed, nor the smell of fire had passed on them.*

28. *Then Nebuchadnezzar spake, and said, Blessed be the God of Shadrach, Meshach, and Abednego, who hath sent his angel, and delivered his servants that trusted in him, and have changed the king's word, and yielded their bodies, that they might not serve nor worship any god, except their own God.*

29. *Therefore I make a decree, That every people, nation, and language, which speak any thing amiss against the God of Shadrach, Meshach, and Abednego, shall be cut in pieces, and their houses shall be made a dunghill: because there is no other God that can deliver after this sort.*

30. *Then the king promoted Shadrach, Meshach, and Abednego, in the province of Babylon.*—Dan. 3:26–30.

We are dealing with one of the most powerful figures in history. Nebuchadnezzar was the builder of one of the ancient wonders of the world. He was considered by his contemporaries as the excellent king of Babylon, ruling 127 provinces from India to Ethiopia. Nobody had the power, the clout, the prestige that Nebuchadnezzar had.

But God has a way of dealing with the "higher ups" as well as the "lower downs." With Him there is no respect of persons. God doesn't respect us for what we have, nor take away from what we are because of what we don't have. He doesn't respect any one person. Before Him, all are guilty. There are only two kinds of sinners—saved and lost.

God is going to deal with Nebuchadnezzar. He will touch his heart, and we will see some exciting things happen. In this message, Nebuchadnezzar will acknowledge who God is.

God is a God of law and order. The more we study space and read about what scientists and astronauts are doing, the more baffled we become with the brilliance, beauty and bounty of all outer reaches of space that man is just now beginning to find. The universal systems, the multiplied billions of stars that are not even in our galaxy, stars much bigger than our sun, are not held in place by accident.

God is a God of law and order. He runs a tight ship. He keeps a perfect record. Our God, acclaimed by Nebuchadnezzar as being the only God who can deliver, as He did in this chapter, created a universe totally controlled by laws.

Some people don't like to be under the restraint of regulations, rules and laws; but we creatures are placed by God the Creator under certain laws. Every member of Adam's race is subject to laws. The birds that fly through the air, the beasts that wander through the fields, the fishes that swim through the sea—all are governed by laws. Laws are inevitable to the ongoing of the universe. Laws are absolutely necessary to our well being. Laws govern and restrict every area of our lives. There is no escape from the moral and spiritual laws that govern God's people.

There is no way to circumvent the laws of science and chemistry. To resist the law is to resist the Lawgiver. You don't just resist a law written in a book; you resist the One who made the law. So to resist one single law of God is to put a fist in God's face and say, "I'm resisting You!" To break a law is to offend the Lawgiver.

God has put in His Word certain inescapable laws. We often think about the Ten Commandments, then stop there. But they are not all the laws. You say, "I've never stolen anything in my life," or "I've never killed anybody," or "I've never committed adultery." But if you are guilty of breaking one law of God, you are guilty of breaking all. Let me read it to you from James 2:10: "For whosoever shall keep the whole law, and yet offend in one point, he is guilty of all." That should bring some silence. You don't have to break all ten; break only one law, and James says you are guilty of all.

We are admonished to obey the laws of the land that govern and guide us. Turn to I Peter 2:13–15 to see what Peter said about it:

"Submit yourselves to every ordinance of man for the Lord's sake: whether it be to the king, as supreme; Or unto governors, as unto them that are sent by him for the punishment of evildoers, and for the praise of them that do well. For so is the

will of God, that with well doing ye may put to silence the ignorance of foolish men."

Peter is saying there are ordinances that govern us. He is saying, in essence, that God is the One who gave the ordinances, the One who established law and the government; and when we resist government, we resist God. He is on His throne in Heaven; we are on earth.

I ask you, Who are we finite creatures down here to try to tell God how to operate His universe? how to operate the world? God is supreme. He set in order everything that is in order.

Turn to Romans 13:1-7. We are talking about being submissive to the laws of the land. I didn't say you will like it—some laws I think are unfair—but God says,

"Let every soul be subject unto the higher powers. For there is no power but of God: the powers that be are ordained of God. Whosoever therefore resisteth the power, resisteth the ordinance of God."

There are some principles here. If we resist the principle of government, we resist God because He established government. Young people, if you resist the authority and law of your parents, you resist God, because God established the home. If you resist pastoral authority and the rules and regulations of the church, you resist God, because He ordained the church. It is important that we understand that.

"Whosoever therefore resisteth the power, resisteth the ordinance of God: and they that resist shall receive to themselves damnation. For rulers are not a terror to good works, but to the evil. Wilt thou then not be afraid of the power? do that which is good, and thou shalt have praise of the same: For he is the minister of God to thee for good. But if thou do that which is evil, be afraid; for he beareth not the sword in vain: for he is the minister of God, a revenger to execute wrath upon him that doeth evil. Wherefore ye must needs be subject, not only for

wrath, but also for conscience sake. For for this cause pay ye
tribute also. . . ."

Probably not a person in this house but can wait until April
15 so you can pay up all your income taxes! But it's the law.
It is also the law to pay your tithe:

"For for this cause pay ye tribute also: for they are God's
ministers, attending continually upon this very thing. Render
therefore to all their dues: tribute to whom tribute is due; cus-
tom to whom custom; fear to whom fear; honour to whom
honour."

The three Hebrew children had to make a decision. The law
of the land said they must bow down. But any law contrary
to the Word of God, to the work of God and to the will of God,
can be circumvented by a Christian. These young men faced
a dilemma. The law of the land said they must bow down. Follow me carefully. Not all laws are righteous. We understand
that. Not all laws are sanctioned by God. We know that. Not
all laws are based on Scripture. We know that. But I want you
to see that the concept, the idea of there being a law in a land
to govern, is of God. It is He who established the principle of
law and order and government.

Here is what I want you to get: Any law contrary to God's
law or any law that violates a principle of Scripture should be
circumvented by Christians.

In Acts 5:29 Peter declared, "We ought to obey God rather
than men." Now when a law violates a scriptural principle or
is contrary to the law of God, then we have to be daring enough
to say, "I can't do it."

The three Hebrew children said, 'We can't bow down and
worship. It's against the law of God.'

What happened? The fiery furnace. But God—but God—
delivered them! God literally changed the law of science by
saying, "Reverse yourself and be cool to My people." Why?

Because they had said, "If we burn, we still are going to do what God says do."

Can we too say, "Regardless of what the world says, or what the Devil says; regardless of what my peers say, what pressure I face, I'll do what God says"?

Even among independent, fundamental, Bible-believing Christians there is a danger of giving in to the world, a danger of saying we're outnumbered. But since when did God need a majority? God plus one is always a majority. There's a danger in our thinking that the world has the upper hand—the money, the energy, the wherewithal, the institutions. Wait a minute! It all belongs to God. It is time to start claiming some of it for God. Let's not give in to the world nor to Satan. "Greater is he that is in you, than he that is in the world."

We are God's children, children of THE King. God abides in us. He owns all the world. We have such anemic faith anymore. When we see the world going on with its program and making all kinds of moves, we sit back and say and do nothing. Let's assert our rights and tell that world, "God made it for us. He wants us to have it."

God will change a law for us, as He did for the Hebrew children.

I. THE LAWS OF BABYLON

Observe three things about the laws of Babylon.

1. *The laws were permanently fixed and final.* Nebuchadnezzar was a tyrant, ruthless, arrogant, proud and discompassionate. But his word was the law of the land. When he spoke, his subjects heeded. And what he commanded was done without question.

But once in awhile there crop up some strange people, like the three Hebrews who said, "We're in your land and subject to you, but we won't bow down to your image." Thank God for any who have the backbone to say, "I'll do what God says, not what you demand."

These laws were fixed and final.

2. *They were universally accepted and obeyed.* We read in chapter 3 how nations bowed down to worship the golden image. People came from far and near to worship Nebuchadnezzar, their god. And those laws were universally obeyed and accepted.

3. *They were sternly enacted and enforced.* Remember what happened in chapter 3? The verses prior to the ones that I read tell how the three Hebrews were thrown into the fiery furnace and that the heat was so intense that the men who threw them in, burned to death. Yet the moment the Hebrews got in the furnace, God changed the laws of chemistry and science, and air-conditioned the inside, so that they came forth without even the smell of smoke. Their hair was not singed nor their clothes burned. The fire had no power on them. Yes, God changed a chemistry law in favor of those who would trust God.

Even if we go into the furnace, God will deliver. But if He doesn't, we still will not worship the golden image.

A lot of people are bowing down to some stupid, sinful images—images of materialism, of lust, of greed, of selfishness. Grabbing and getting. When someone asked John D. Rockefeller, "How much money does it take to satisfy a man?" he answered, "One more dollar." Bowing down at the altar of greed, of materialism—don't do it!

In spite of the universality, the severity or the permanency of Nebuchadnezzar's laws, they could be changed—indeed, were changed by the God of the universe, changed in favor of a higher law—the law of God.

II. THE LAWS OF GOD

What about the laws of God? They are eternal. They don't start and stop here. They are eternal in existence, irrevocable, incomparable, inviolable, inescapable and impartial. The laws of God are ordained in Heaven. The laws of God are superior to the laws of man. The laws of God are forever fixed and permanently unchangeable.

Now here's a question, and this is the crux of my message: Why would God change the laws of a worldwide empire and the laws of nature that He Himself had put into operation, to accommodate three young men? Because His integrity, His Word and His own person were at stake.

God will do whatever is necessary to preserve His integrity. He will do whatever is necessary to promote His work. He will do whatever is necessary to protect His people. In this case, He changed the laws in order to protect three relatively unknown young men.

We see that God is constantly in tune with the goings on down here. He's not asleep. He's not an absentee from the classroom of man's activities. God doesn't wake up to surprises. I quote a famous preacher: "Has it ever occurred to you that it never occurred to God?" He has never had a surprise. He doesn't wake up of a morning—the God of Abraham, Isaac and Jacob never sleeps. His eyes are ever open to our needs. He knows what is taking place. He knows all His creatures, all His people.

Scientists tell us that with the naked eye the average person can see something like thirty thousand stars out of the billions and billions in the sky. That is no exaggeration.

This reminds me of the story of the preacher who was given to exaggeration. After a few months, the men of the church came to him and said, "Now preacher, we've got to do something. You exaggerate too much. You overstate things." He answered, "I know. I've shed billions and billions of tears over that very thing."

There are literally billions of stars out there. And you know what? God has given a name to each. "He telleth the number of the stars; he calleth them all by their names" (Ps. 147:4).

We know the Morning Star, the Evening Star, and star light and star bright; but God knows them all by name. Can you imagine that! Science books will tell you there are billions of stars that have never been seen, yet God knows every one of them.

If God knows every star by name, don't you think He knows your name? Jesus said, "My sheep hear my voice, and I know them . . . ."

God knows who you are, where you live, where you work. He knows your house number, your employment number, your telephone number, your area code, your zip code, your Social Security number, your bank account number. He knows your pulse rate, your heartbeat. He knows the motives of your heart. He knows your plans, your intentions, your desires, your drives, your ambitions. He knows what bothers you, what concerns you, what threatens you. He knows your blood pressure, your bank balance. He knows your trials, temptations, troubles, heartaches, afflictions, sorrows and your difficulties. Somewhere in Scripture it says God knows even the number of the hairs on your head. Somewhere in Scripture it says that even a sparrow falling is acknowledged by God. If He acknowledges every little flower that withers up out there in the hot sun; if He knows every star by name; if He makes note of every fallen sparrow, surely He keeps track of His own people. How much more important are you than many sparrows! Job said in 23:10, "But he knoweth the way that I take: when he hath tried me, I shall come forth as gold."

Verse 28 of chapter 3 in Daniel says God sent His angel. God won't spare a thing to protect His people. I read in Psalm 34:7, "The angel of the Lord encampeth round about them that fear him, and delivereth them."

He sent His angel to deliver His servants. He changed the laws of the land. The same God who delivered the Hebrew children from the fiery furnace can deliver you, because "God is no respecter of persons" (Acts 10:34). What He did for others, He'll do for you.

You say, "The day of miracles is over." Who said? I just had a miracle—breathing. I just batted my eye—a miracle. Some of you stayed awake during this sermon—a miracle! The world is full of miracles. We don't see them because we are not looking for them. We really doubt whether God can perform miracles anymore. We've left it to the Pentecostals and the charismatics. My daddy said fifty years ago, "If Baptists had been what they should have been, there would never have been a Pentecostal movement."

When in seminary forty years ago, a very popular song among the student body was:

> **It is no secret what God can do;**
> **What He's done for others, He'll do for you;**
> **With arms wide open, He'll pardon you;**
> **It is no secret what God can do.**

What is your fiery furnace? your furnace of affliction? If God can change a heathen king and kingdom and the laws of a worldwide empire, certainly He can change your circumstances. Let's begin to believe God for some miracles.

Some of you are bound financially. Some of you are emotionally bound in prison. Some of you are at a standstill spiritually. Why don't you let God change what seems unchangeable? Let Him put out the fires of your fiery furnace. Let Him cut asunder the cords that bind you and break down the walls that imprison you. Let Him perform a miracle of grace for you. It is no secret what God can do. What He's done for others, He can do for you.

Seven Years of Wild Living

Introduction

Man and God are worlds apart. A deadly disease called sin has driven a wedge between them—Isaiah 59:1, 2.

NOTE: On the one hand is a holy and righteous God; on the other hand is sinful and rebellious man.

- Man at his **best is bad**.
- Man at his **strongest is weak**.
- Man at his **wisest is unwise**.

NOTE: We have no right to boast or brag about **who** we are, what we **know**, or what we **have**.

COMMENTARY: Jeremiah 9:23, 24

NOTE: Nebuchadnezzar is a prime example of the truth stated in Proverbs 16:18—"Pride goeth...."

Warning: I Corinthians 10:12—"Let him that...."
Proverbs 6:16–19

Someone observed: "Pride is number one on God's **hate** parade."

I Peter 5:5—*"God resisteth the proud..."*

NOTE: Nebuchadnezzar was like an island:

- Self on North
- Self on South
- Self on East
- Self on West

Poem: "I Had a Little Tea Party"

NOTE: Look at this man, this powerful king:
—puffed up
—proud
—conceited
—egotistical
—stubborn
—rebellious
—obstinate
—arrogant

Beside all that: some sort of mental illness (many world leaders have)

NOTE: Plagued with "I" disease: I, my, mine (Someone said he had a bad case of "perpendicular-'i'tis.")

Actually a form of hysteria—"manic-depressive"
- "gloom or glow"
- "up or down"
- moods: high/low

It has been suggested that hysteria expresses itself in 3 ways (Nebuchadnezzar had all 3):

1. Emotionalism—"raging maniac" at times
2. Amnesia—7 years
3. Egotism—image (Chapter 2)

NOTE: Lessons to learn from this experience of King Nebuchadnezzar: verse 17

1. God rules in the kingdoms of men.
2. God gives power to whomsoever He will.
3. God puts base men in positions of power.

   - God has not removed Himself from national affairs.
   - He is still in control.
   - America is destined for judgment.
   - Russian Pastor V. Zinchenko's statement.

Message

> **NOTE:** Nebuchadnezzar was made to live like a wild man for seven years for three reasons:
>
> (By the way, he had a whole year of grace—verse 29, Ecclesiastes 8:11–13.)

I. HE REFUSED TO OBEY THE WORD OF GOD.

> **NOTE:** 4:24–27
> **OBSERVE:** Verse 27; Proverbs 28:13
> **COMMENT:** Obey God's Word.

II. HE ATTEMPTED TO OPERATE HIS LIFE AND HIS KINGDOM INDEPENDENTLY OF GOD.

> **NOTE:** Verse 30a
>
> **ILLUSTRATION:** Rich man—Luke 16 (I, my, mine)
>
> **ILLUSTRATION:** Man jumped from 25-story building. Someone asked the custodian of the building why he did it.
>
> *Answer:* "When a man leaves God out of his life, there's nothing left for him to do but jump."

III. HE FAILED TO GIVE GOD THE GLORY.

> **NOTE:** Verse 30b
> - Failed to recognize that it was God who gave him the kingdom and made him who he was
> - Daniel 2:37, 38
> - I Corinthians 4:7
>
> **ILLUSTRATION:** Herod Agrippa I—Acts 12:24

CHAPTER EIGHT

 Seven Years of Wild Living

28. *All this came upon the king Nebuchadnezzar.*

29. *At the end of twelve months he walked in the palace of the kingdom of Babylon.* [Now watch this].

30. *The king spake, and said, Is not this great Babylon, that I have built for the house of the kingdom by the might of my power, and for the honour of my majesty?*

31. *While the word was in the king's mouth, there fell a voice from heaven, saying, O king Nebuchadnezzar, to thee it is spoken; The kingdom is departed from thee.*

32. *And they shall drive thee from men, and thy dwelling shall be with the beasts of the field: they shall make thee to eat grass as oxen, and seven times shall pass over thee, until thou know that the most High ruleth in the kingdom of men, and giveth it to whomsoever he will.*

33. *The same hour was the thing fulfilled upon Nebuchad-nezzar: and he was driven from men, and did eat grass as oxen, and his body was wet with the dew of heaven, till his hairs were grown like eagles' feathers, and his nails like birds' claws.—* Dan. 4:28–33.

Nebuchadnezzar begins what we know, in the period of

biblical history, as the *"Times of the Gentiles."* His reign—from about 626 to about 562 B.C.—was a reign of terror. This man was a schizophrenic. He had a split personality. Out of the pages of history comes the record of his mental illness. We shall speak more about that in a moment.

But in the opening of chapter 4, Nebuchadnezzar relates an unusual dream, a dream about a tree that grew large and tall and reached unto the heavens and spread its lofty boughs across the whole earth. Its fruit was plenteous.

The tree was so large that even the beasts could come and find shelter, perhaps from lightning and storms. The birds of the air could make their nests there. It was an enormous tree.

In that dream there comes from Heaven a messenger called the "Holy One" in the text. The messenger, the Holy One, comes and says about this tree, 'Hew [cut] it down but not all the way down. Leave the stump. And put a band of iron and brass around it. And let it be wet with the dew of heaven because it will come back again.'

Nebuchadnezzar called all the wise men, as he did after his dream in chapter 2, but none could decipher nor interpret that dream. Then comes Daniel. He by this time had perhaps become a rather good friend, if I might put it in those terms, of this king. When he heard about the dream, verse 19 says, "Then Daniel, whose name was Belteshazzar [don't confuse that name with Belshazzar, the great grandson of Nebuchadnezzar], was astonied for one hour, and his thoughts troubled him."

Later on he interprets that dream and tells the king exactly what it meant. In a nutshell, the dream meant that the kingdom of Nebuchadnezzar, the kingdom of the Chaldeans, the Babylonians, his excellency, one of the greatest kings ever to rule a world empire, would be removed, his kingdom taken away and he would be cut down. Verse 28 says, "All this came upon the king Nebuchadnezzar."

What "came upon" him? He was driven into the wilderness

to live like a beast for seven years. He was out of his mind, out of control—but all in the plan of Almighty God.

Man and God are worlds apart. The natural man perceiveth not the things of God. He discerneth not spiritual things. Paul says he cannot know spiritual things because spiritual things are spiritually discerned, and man's mind by nature is against God. Don't think that man is a goody-goody; he is by nature a sinner. "For all have sinned, and come short of the glory of God." "There is none righteous, no, not one." "There is none that doeth good, no, not one." By nature man has gone astray. The psalmist said that "as soon as they be born [they speak] lies."

Did you have to teach your child to tell a lie? No. You had to teach him how to tell the truth. I would like to teach some adults how, too. Be honest. Have integrity. Man and God are worlds apart because of a deadly malady, a disease which the Bible calls sin. Man has transgressed God's law. Sin has driven a wedge between God and man.

On the one hand is a holy and righteous God; on the other, a selfish, sinful, sensual, rebellious, obstinate man. Man at best is bad, bad. Paul says that within this flesh dwelleth no good thing. Man at his strongest is weak; man at his wisest is very unwise. We have no right to boast or brag about WHO we are or WHAT we have or what we can DO or what we KNOW. If we must boast, let it be in Jesus. Paul wrote in Galatians 6:14, "But God forbid that I should glory [boast], save in the cross of our Lord Jesus Christ, by whom the world is crucified unto me, and I unto the world." Don't brag about who you are, where you have been, where you are going, what you know or what you have.

Jeremiah 9:23, 24 admonishes:

"Let not the wise man glory in his wisdom, neither let the mighty man glory in his might, let not the rich man glory in

his riches: But let him that glorieth glory in this, that he under-
standeth and knoweth me. . . . "

The only thing we can brag about is that we know who God
is. Do you know Him? Do you know Him in the pardon and
forgiveness of your sin? Do you have an intimate relationship
with Christ? Can you say, "The King and I walk down life's road
together"?

*". . . that he understandeth and knoweth me, that I am the
Lord which exercise lovingkindness, judgment, and righteousness, in the earth: for in these things I delight, saith the Lord."*

Nebuchadnezzar is a prime example of the truth stated in
Proverbs 16:18, "Pride goeth before destruction, and an haughty
spirit before a fall." And in I Corinthians 10:12 Paul warns,
"Wherefore let him that thinketh he standeth take heed lest
he fall." And in Proverbs 6:16–19 wise Solomon tells us:

*"These six things doth the Lord hate: yea, seven are an abomi-
nation unto him: A proud look, a lying tongue, and hands that
shed innocent blood, An heart that deviseth wicked imagina-
tions, feet that be swift in running to mischief, A false witness
that speaketh lies, and he that soweth discord among brethren."*

Of the seven things God hates, number one is a proud look.
In I Peter 5:5 we read, ". . . for God resisteth the proud, and
giveth grace to the humble."

Nebuchadnezzar was like an island: *self* on the North, *self*
on the South, *self* on the East, and *self* on the West.

The poet said,

> **I had a little tea party**
> **This afternoon at three.**
> **'Twas very small, three guests in all—**
> **I, Myself and Me.**
> **Myself ate all the sandwiches,**
> **While I drank all the tea;**
> **'Twas also I that ate the pie,**
> **And passed the cake to Me.**

Some people are just that wrapped up in self. A person wrapped up in himself makes a mighty small package. The most miserable person is he who cannot see beyond self. If you tell him about a need, a burden or a problem, he has one bigger, and he cannot wait to tell you about it—thinking only of self.

Nebuchadnezzar was puffed up. This powerful king was proud, conceited, egotistical, stubborn, rebellious, obstinate, arrogant and ambitious. Besides, he had some kind of mental illness. Many world leaders have that. I've been told that anybody with leadership qualities has a little mental quirk, a mental disease.

Nebuchadnezzar had a split personality. He was a schizophrenic. In fact, the authorities tell us that he probably suffered from some form of hysteria. He was plagued with "I" disease. And I don't mean the kind that glasses can correct. Someone suggested that he had a bad case of "perpendicular-'i'tis." Actually, it was a form of hysteria. He was a manic depressive—all gloom or all glow. Way up or way down. His mood swung from high to low—on top or at the bottom.

Hysteria (and authorities will bear this out) expresses itself in three different ways. *Emotionalism:* this was characteristic of Nebuchadnezzar—a raging maniac at times. *Amnesia:* for seven years he didn't know who he was. *Egotism:* any man who would make an image and try to get everybody to bow down and worship it has a king-sized ego problem.

Here is a man suffering from hysteria, a king who had to learn three basic lessons that each one of us ought to learn. Chapter 4, verse 17: "This matter is by the decree of the watchers, and the demand by the word of the holy ones: to the intent that the living may know...."

Now here are the lessons that we need to learn: (1) God rules in the kingdom of men; (2) God gives power to whomsoever He will; (3) God puts base men in positions of power. Study world leaders, heads of nations and states; some are of the basest sort.

I ought to tell you that God has not removed Himself from national affairs. He knows what is going on in our nation. God is still in control. And America is destined for God's judgment. While churches are empty, so-called Christians are taking to the highways of pleasure, taking care of business or sitting home watching television. Don't tell me the judgment of God is not now on America!

I shuddered when Brother Zinchenko, our Russian pastor, said to me and my wife, "America deserves the judgment of God more than Russia." That sort of upset me at first; but then America, with all of her enlightenment, with all of our churches and church-related institutions, with all of our opportunities of enlightenment, education and religion, does deserve God's judgment more than an atheistic nation. Those people have never known the truth. We've had the truth, and we've made fun of the truth. We've neglected the truth, abused the truth. We've abused our privileges of worship. We've neglected God's house. We've turned a deaf ear to God. Yes, America does deserve judgment more than Russia.

When are we going to learn that we cannot keep on neglecting God and His house, turning a deaf ear to His call, and neglecting our responsibilities as Christians in the Sunday school, in the church ministry—when are we going to learn that we Americans cannot continue to do that without having the judgment of God fall on us?

And I have an idea that God is sick to His stomach of all the flimsy excuses that we give for not serving Him.

My message is entitled "Seven Years of Wild Living" or "The Man Who Lived Seven Years Like an Animal." Nebuchadnezzar was made to live like a wild man, like a beast, for seven years for three reasons.

Verse 29: "At the end of twelve months . . . ." I conclude from this verse that after Nebuchadnezzar had the dream and after Daniel had interpreted it—that his kingdom would be cut off, like a tree cut down with just a stump left in the ground—that the king had a full year to repent, to get right with God, but he didn't. Turn to Ecclesiastes, chapter 8, and see that, even when God gives a grace period to men, they won't repent.

"Because sentence against an evil work is not executed speedily, therefore the heart of the sons of men is fully set in them to do evil. Though a sinner do evil an hundred times, and his days be prolonged, yet surely I know that it shall be well with them that fear God, which fear before him: But it shall not be well with the wicked, neither shall he prolong his days, which are as a shadow; because he feareth not before God."—Vss. 11-13.

Nebuchadnezzar had twelve full months to make things right with God. Here is a man who had risen to power, who was prominent, powerful and proud, who was egotistical, arrogant and rebellious, who was ambitious and who had sinned against God. The sentence had already come on him, that he would live like an animal for seven years. And God gave him a whole year to get right.

God has also given us long enough to get right with Him. He has extended His mercy to America long enough for her to repent. But one day His patience will wear out.

> **There is a time, I know not when,**
> **A place, I know not where,**
> **That marks the destiny of men**
> **To Heaven or despair.**

Since God is a God of mercy, He always acts in mercy before He acts in judgment.

Nebuchadnezzar's twelve months had now run out. "At the end of twelve months he walked in the palace of the kingdom of Babylon."

There are three reasons why this man had to live for

seven long years in the wilds, like an animal.

I. HE REFUSED TO OBEY GOD'S WORD

24. *This is the interpretation, O king, and this is the decree of the most High, which is come upon my lord the king:*

25. *That they shall drive thee from men, and thy dwelling shall be with the beasts of the field, and they shall make thee to eat grass as oxen, and they shall wet thee with the dew of heaven, and seven times* [seven years. A time is a year in Daniel's writing.] *shall pass over thee, till thou know that the most High ruleth in the kingdom of men, and giveth it to whomsoever he will.*

26. *And whereas they commanded to leave the stump of the tree roots; thy kingdom shall be sure unto thee, after that thou shalt have known that the heavens do rule.*

27. *Wherefore, O king, let my counsel be acceptable unto thee, and break off thy sins by righteousness, and thine iniquities by shewing mercy to the poor; if it may be a lengthening of thy tranquillity.*—Dan. 4:24–27.

Remember the lesson Nebuchadnezzar had to learn and the lesson we must learn: God is in charge, in control. The heavens rule the earth. God is on His throne. He is not struggling for power; He already has it. He is in authority.

Verse 27: "Wherefore, O king, let my counsel be acceptable unto thee, and break off thy sins by righteousness, and thine iniquities by shewing mercy to the poor; if it may be a lengthening of thy tranquillity."

Listen! Nebuchadnezzar had to live like a wild man for seven years, with hair growing on his body like feathers, claws coming out like eagles' claws, being wet with the dew of Heaven and eating grass like oxen, all because he refused to obey the Word of God. He would not forsake nor repent nor confess his sins and ask for forgiveness.

The wise Solomon says in Proverbs 28:13, "He that covereth his sins shall not prosper: but whoso confesseth and forsaketh them shall have mercy."

Have you come to the place where you can say, "God, whatever You say, I'll obey. If You say China, I will go to China. If You say Mexico, I'll go to Mexico. If You say teach a class, I'll teach. If You say drive a bus, I will do that. If You say sing in the choir, I'll sing. If You say win souls, win souls I will do. If You say tithe, I'll tithe. If You say visit the homeless, the sick, the poor, the needy, I'll do all of that. I'll do whatever You say do"?

Don't be guilty of disobeying the Word of God. To obey is better than sacrifice. Jesus said, "If you love me, keep my commandments."

The king lived in the wilds for seven years like an animal, losing his mind, his control, his respect—losing everything because he refused to obey God.

Am I speaking to some tonight who really haven't obeyed God? You are saved, and you have come this far. You have done this and that, but God tells you to do this and do this and do this. "No, God, I can't do it. I have a business, a family, a home. I have ambitions." But God commands, "Do it!"

The consequences are altogether too severe when one disobeys the Word of God.

II. HE OPERATED INDEPENDENTLY OF GOD

Nebuchadnezzar lived like a wild man because he attempted to operate his life and kingdom independently of God. No one can do that. You can't operate your business nor work your job independently of Him.

Here is a man who tried to.

Look again at the first part of verse 30. That day he walked out in his palace and said, 'Is not this great Babylon that I have built? Isn't this the kingdom of all kingdoms? Isn't this the finest kingdom in all the world that I have built?'

He had done no such thing! The rich man in the New Testament, recorded in Luke 12, said, 'Because I have no room where to bestow my fruits. . . . I will pull down my barns and build greater. . . . I will say to my soul, Soul, thou hast much goods laid up for many years. . . soul, take it easy. Soul, rest.'

But that very night, like a bolt of lightning, the voice of God said, "Thou fool, this night thy soul shall be required of thee: then whose shall those things be, which thou hast provided?"

God help us to get the right perspective. Jesus said, "For without me ye can do nothing." Nebuchadnezzar said, 'Is not this the great kingdom that stretches from India to Ethiopia, 127 provinces, that I, I, Nebuchadnezzar, have built?'

I read where a wealthy man jumped from the twenty-fifth floor window in Chicago and splattered his life on the sidewalk below. When someone asked the janitor of that building, "Why do you suppose he jumped?" he said, "Mister, when a man leaves God out of his life, nothing is left but to jump."

Young people, if you're leaving God out of your plan, going your way, doing your own thing, there is nothing else left to do but jump.

III. HE FAILED TO GIVE GOD THE GLORY

Nebuchadnezzar lived like a wild man because, not only did he refuse to obey the Word of God and attempt to operate his life and kingdom independently of God, but he failed to give God the glory.

This is a dangerous thing. God would do more for us if we praised Him for what He has already done. You think you've got it bad, think the world is on top of you, think you have it hard, think you are lonely?

Come with me. The last couple of days I visited nine nursing homes where we have ten, twelve, fourteen people. I left every room pushing back the tears. These people are lonely, hurting. These people need somebody to visit them. You and I don't have much to complain about. Nor do we have much to brag about. To God alone be the glory! God forbid that I should glory save in the cross of our Lord Jesus Christ.

Nebuchadnezzar failed to give God the glory. Look at verse 30 of chapter 4. In the first part he said, "I have . . . ." In the last part we read, ". . . for the house of the kingdom by the might of my power, and for the honour of my majesty." He failed to recognize that God had given him everything he had.

Turn back to chapter 2, verses 37, 38. This is when Daniel interpreted that other dream that Nebuchadnezzzar had.

"Thou, O king, art a king of kings: for the God of heaven hath given thee a kingdom, power, and strength, and glory. And wheresoever the children of men dwell, the beasts of the field and the fowls of the heaven hath he given into thine hand, and hath made thee ruler over them all."

Nebuchadnezzar was bragging, "I have built it. I have accumulated it. I have gathered it. I have done it with my power, with my might, with my honor, with my majesty." The truth is, he had done nothing. God had given him everything.

Whatever we have, God has given to us. The breath we breathe, the life we have—we didn't get it on our own.

In I Corinthians 4:7 Paul had just been talking about being puffed up one against another. "For who maketh thee to differ from another? and what hast thou that thou didst not receive? now if thou didst receive it, why dost thou glory, as if thou hadst not received it?"

Let us never say, "I have done it. I have accumulated it." Where did you get the breath to breathe? the energy to go on? those precious children? God gave it all. God gives everything, owns everything. And isn't it gracious of Him to share with us out of the riches of His glory!

Let me give you one stern warning from the Bible.

Turn to Acts 12. It is dangerous not to give God the glory. King Agrippa I, grandson of Herod the Great, was on his throne. He was somebody. He had it made. He was dressed up in all of his rich apparel. Verses 21–23:

"And upon a set day Herod [Herod Agrippa I], *arrayed in royal apparel, sat upon his throne, and made an oration* [a great speech] *unto them. And the people gave a shout, saying, It is the voice of a God, and not of a man. And immediately the angel of the Lord smote him.* [Why? Because he made a speech? No. Because of what the speech said? No.] *The angel of the Lord smote him because he gave not God the glory: and he was eaten of worms."*

Can you imagine a more horrible death! You are sitting on your throne or in your front room or in the church pew or in your car. All of a sudden little creepy creatures start from your toenails and go up to your fingernails and get in your eyes and ears and mouth—all over your body—until all your flesh is eaten away. You are sitting there as a skeleton. Those little worms are scratching at your skeleton now that your flesh is gone. Worms have an insatiable appetite.

God smote him with worms. Why? Because he gave not God the glory. And the Bible says, ". . . and he gave up the ghost." When worms have destroyed you, it is about time to give up the ghost.

Look at Acts 12:24: "But the word of God grew and multiplied."

The old Book will still be going when this old world is on fire.

—— *Outline* 4:34–37 ——

A Man in His Right Mind

Introduction

General remarks: Nebuchadnezzar—what a character! What a study in contrasts!

- Lived like a beast for seven years because of his pride: "Is not this **great** Babylon that **I** have built... **my** power ... **my** majesty?"
- During exile—time to rethink, reevaluate, reassess his entire life
- God worked a miracle of grace in his life.

> **NOTE:** God did something to Nebuchadnezzar that resulted in bringing glory to Himself.
>
> **APPLY:** Your life and mine (Rom. 8:28)
>
> **ILLUSTRATION:** Fanny Crosby: blindness/spiritual sight

Message

I. HOW DID NEBUCHADNEZZAR GET HIS RIGHT MIND BACK?

> **NOTE:** Verse 34a (Psalm 121:1)
> Verse 36a
>
> **NOTE:** We look to God.
> 1. Help in time of **trouble**—Psalm 46:1; 121:1
> 2. Direction in running life's **race**—Heb. 12:1, 2
> 3. **Salvation** of our souls—Isaiah 45:22

> **NOTE:** Sin is spiritual insanity.
> Classic example: prodigal son
> • "Hogpen hiatus"
> • Beside himself: "slime and slum"
> • *"When he **came** to himself...."*
>
> **NOTE:** Most insane people on earth: Devil's crowd
> Most sensible people on earth: God's people

II. WHAT DID NEBUCHADNEZZAR DO WHEN HE GOT HIS RIGHT MIND BACK?

He made an about-face/total change.

- All his bewilderment turned into blessing.
- All his frustrations were resolved.
- All his fears were allayed.
- He regained his self-esteem.

He is now a man in control/new man. No longer does he crawl like a beast.

1. Acknowledged that God alone is to be praised—34a
2. Acknowledged the eternality of God's kingdom—34b
3. Acknowledged that man is nothing without God—35a
4. Acknowledged that none can prevent God from exercising His will—35b

> **NOTE:** Don't ask God what He is doing!
> **NOTE:** Romans 11:33–36—*"O the depth...."*
> **NOTE:** "This Is My Father's World"

5. Acknowledged that God is true and just—37a
6. Acknowledged that God can bring down the proud—37b
    - Luke 18:14—*"Every one that exalteth..."*
    - Proverbs 16:18—*"Pride goeth before..."*
    - I Peter 5:5, 6—*"God resisteth the proud..."*

- James 4:6—(Same thing Peter said:) *"God resisteth...."*

> **NOTE:** Getting back to God did something for Nebuchadnezzar.
> 1. Improved his **looks**—verse 36 (brightness)
> 2. Enhanced his **position**—verse 36 (established)
>
> **NOTE:** Getting right with God: best thing you can do

III. HOW DID NEBUCHADNEZZAR'S BEHAVIOR AFFECT THOSE ABOUT HIM WHEN HE GOT HIS RIGHT MIND BACK?

They reestablished their relationship—verse 36.

> **NOTE:** Your state of mind and status in life will affect those around you.
>
> **NOTE:** Paul said we can't live nor die without affecting others—Romans 14:7.
> 1. When you and I **serve God**, we influence others.
> 2. When we **witness**, we influence others.
> 3. When we **pray**, we influence others.
> 4. When we **give**, we influence others.
> 5. When we **attend church**, we influence others.
> 6. When we **do right**, we influence others.
> 7. When we **praise God**, we influence others.
>
> **BOTTOM LINE:** When we are **where** we ought to be with God, others will want to be **where** we **are**!

Conclusion

Where are you with God—scale of one to ten?

> **NOTE:** Five cylinders: prayer, Bible study, giving, attendance, witnessing

Appeal: Come closer at an altar of prayer, and improve your relationship with God.

CHAPTER NINE

A Man in His Right Mind

34. *And at the end of the days I Nebuchadnezzar lifted up mine eyes unto heaven, and mine understanding returned unto me, and I blessed the most High, and I praised and honoured him that liveth for ever, whose dominion is an everlasting dominion, and his kingdom is from generation to generation:*

35. *And all the inhabitants of the earth are reputed as nothing: and he doeth according to his will in the army of heaven, and among the inhabitants of the earth: and none can stay his hand, or say unto him, What doest thou?*

36. *At the same time my reason returned unto me; and for the glory of my kingdom, mine honour and brightness returned unto me; and my counsellors and my lords sought unto me; and I was established in my kingdom, and excellent majesty was added unto me.*

37. *Now I Nebuchadnezzar praise and extol and honour the King of heaven, all whose works are truth, and his ways judgment: and those that walk in pride he is able to abase.*—Dan. 4:34–37.

Nebuchadnezzar: the name means *defender of the boundary.* Nobody had more to defend than he. The great kingdom of the Babylonians consisted of 127 provinces that stretched from India to Ethiopia. From 606 to 562 B.C. he ruled with a rod of iron. There was a lapse in his life. (By the way, there come lapses in the lives of most of us in one way or another.) But he recovered.

Nebuchadnezzar was an unusual man. He built the Hanging Gardens of Babylon, often described as one of the seven wonders of the ancient world. What a man! What a king! What a character! What a study in contrast! He lived like a beast for seven years. This man had his dwelling, literally, in the wilderness on the plains of Shinar. Like a beast, he crawled on all fours. His fingernails and toenails grew out like claws of a wild, ravenous bird. The hair on his body was like feathers. He ate straw like an ox for seven years. Why? Because he failed to give God the glory that rightfully belonged to Him. The book of Revelation tells us that all power, riches, wisdom, strength, honor, glory and blessing belong to God.

In the twentieth century, men have also tried to take that which belongs to God. When we do, we write a prescription for misery, for heartache, for trouble and, ultimately, for destruction.

All blessing, all honor, all glory belong to Him.

Nebuchadnezzar stood and looked over his great kingdom of 127 provinces and said:

30. *Is not this great Babylon, that I have built for the house of the kingdom by the might of my power, and for the honour of my majesty?*

While the king spoke, a voice from Heaven said,

31. *O king Nebuchadnezzar, to thee it is spoken; The kingdom is departed from thee.*

32. *And they shall drive thee from men, and thy dwelling shall be with the beasts of the field: they shall make thee to eat grass as oxen, and seven times shall pass over thee, until*

thou know that the most High ruleth in the kingdom of men, and giveth it to whomsoever he will.

Immediately Nebuchadnezzar started chewing grass and scratching his head with long fingernails and pulling at the feathers that had grown on his body (vs. 33).

His exile was a time of reevaluation, a rethinking of his whole life.

Every once in awhile we need that. I'm not suggesting that we go out and live like animals, but we occasionally need to reevaluate our lives. *Who am I? What is my destiny? What am I doing here? Where am I going? Why am I doing what I am doing? What is my life all about?*

As Nebuchadnezzar reassessed his life, God worked in him a miracle of grace.

God wants to do the same for us. If you are unsaved, the greatest miracle God can perform is salvation for your soul. It took a miracle to put the stars out in space. It took a miracle to put the moon, sun and all those planets in place. This morning early I went outside and saw the beautiful, majestic sunrise. How beautiful the sky was! I saw the Little Dipper, the Milky Way, Mars and others. When I saw a bright star in the East, a brilliant star, I thought of the Wise Men who said, "We have seen his star in the east, and are come to worship him." Wise men are still doing the same.

Tonight I am looking into the faces of some of the wisest people on earth. You may not have gotten the best grades, but still you are wise. You have chosen the better thing—to be in God's house. What better place from which to go to Heaven! Should the trumpet sound in the next five minutes, would you be ready? You say, "Well, I'm in church." But that doesn't mean you are saved. But you can get ready for that trumpet sound sitting right there in the pew. You don't have to write out a prescription or memorize a lot of Scripture or learn the catechism. Just ask Jesus to come into your heart and trust Him, and God will save you right now.

What God did for Nebuchadnezzar resulted in glory to God's own name.

Let me apply that in your life. Everything that happens—sickness, sorrow, death, divorce, debts, destruction—is for your good and God's glory.

Enter Fanny Crosby, the blind hymn writer. In her autobiography she mentions the doctor who, through some mistake, caused her to go blind at birth. When someone asked her one day, "Do you hate that doctor who caused your blindness?" her reply was, "Oh, no. I wish I could find him to thank him. For in my physical blindness, God gave me spiritual light."

Fanny Crosby wrote scores of beautiful hymns which we sing and love today. God gave her spiritual sight to write them, and she thanked God for her blindness.

Thank God for your blindness, for your deafness, for your dumbness. Everybody is not smart about everything. Everybody is stupid about something. Thank God for whatever comes, because He is weaving a pattern for you, out of which He will ultimately get glory.

"A Man in His Right Mind." Three things I want us to consider.

I. HOW DID HE RECOVER HIS MIND?

The answer is stated in verses 34 through 36, which we read at the beginning. The king said, "And at the end of the days [seven years of exile, seven years of abandonment to the wild as an animal] I . . . lifted up mine eyes unto heaven, and mine understanding returned unto me. . . . At the same time my reason returned unto me."

His reasoning came back, and he got his right mind back by looking to God.

Friend, look to God tonight in your time of trouble. Some

of you are going through some very troubled waters. But there is a bridge over those troubled waters—Christ Jesus; and with outstretched hands, He is reaching for you. Look to Him. Depend on Him.

Psalm 46:1 gives the comforting word: "God is our refuge and strength, a very present help in trouble." Not a distant help, not a way off in the sweet by and by, not sometime in yonder's wonderland somewhere—but a very *present* help in time of trouble.

(By the way, don't trouble trouble till trouble troubles you, for you only make your trouble double trouble when you do.)

All have troubles, trials and tribulations. Job reminds us in 14:1, "Man that is born of a woman is of few days, and full of trouble." And again in 5:7, "Yet man is born unto trouble, as the sparks fly upward."

Is there anyone here without trouble? Is there anyone here who doesn't anticipate some trouble? If so, I want to meet you and see where you came from. All have some trouble. But God is our very *present* help in trouble.

Look to Him for direction. Which way are you running? How are you running? In Hebrews 12 Paul said, "Wherefore seeing we also are compassed about with so great a cloud of witnesses, let us lay aside every weight, and the sin which doth so easily beset us, and let us run with patience the race that is set before us, Looking unto Jesus the author and finisher of our faith."

Who are those witnesses? All who have gone on before us are looking down upon us and rooting for us. God's cheering squad is cheering us on.

God will tell you how to run, give you strength to run, and put you running in the right path and the right direction and for the right reason. So look to Him for direction in running the race of life.

On a cold and snowy day in a little province in the country of England, a young man went to a mission church. Since the pastor was ill, a substitute stood up, just a layman out of the congregation, and read Isaiah 45:22, "Look unto me, and be ye saved, all the ends of the earth: for I am God, and there is none else." When he gave an invitation, who stepped out? A young boy by the name of Charles Haddon Spurgeon, later called the "Prince of Preachers."

"Look unto me." "Look and live." "Look to the Lamb of God." "Look unto Jesus, the author and finisher of our faith."

The psalmist vowed, "I will lift up mine eyes unto the hills, from whence cometh my help. My help cometh from the Lord, which made heaven and earth." If He can make Heaven and earth, then He can make your soul a repository of righteousness.

Sin is spiritual insanity. Take a classic example—the prodigal son. He had a notorious case of "hog-pen-itis." I mean he was in a bad shape. In fact, he was "beside himself." The slime, the slum, the scum made him a bum.

There he was in the hogpen. Can you imagine how he looked? As he leaned upon the fence rail that enclosed the hogs, his elbows may have been coming out of his sleeves. He had pawned off his sandals, so he had no shoes. His clothes had the stench of a hogpen. Then all of a sudden he "came to himself." That suggests that he had been outside, or beside, himself.

When we see someone a little flakier than we are, we say, "He's beside himself." That's another way of saying that he has lost his marbles, he is out of his mind, out of control. "And when he came to himself, he said, How many hired servants of my father's have bread enough and to spare, and I perish with hunger?"

Did he say, "I will arise and go to the Welfare system"? No. Did he say, "I will arise and go to HUD"? No. "I will arise and go to my father, and will say unto him, Father, I have sinned against heaven, and before thee, And am no more worthy to be called thy son: make me as one of thy hired servants."

The prodigal starts home. Now he is beginning to get control of himself. (When a man gets control back in his mind and life, he heads toward home.)

Young people, listen! You think Mom and Dad are hard on you, that they come down so many times on you, that they are not fair and are just old fogies. Well, in that case, why don't you pack up your things and head for the hogpen and learn something?

When the prodigal came to himself, he said, "I'm headin' for home!"

All the way home, he memorized his little speech: "Father, I have sinned against heaven, and before thee, And am no more worthy to be called thy son: make me as one of thy hired servants." "Make me a hired servant"—he wanted to make certain he got that right: "Make me a hired servant. . .Make me a hired servant. . .Make me a hired servant."

But when he got in sight of home—guess what! Daddy was out looking. Did the Bible say his daddy ran and took off his belt and whipped him good before he had a chance to say a word? No. Did his dad reprimand him? No. Did his dad say, "Where have you been, young man?" No, no. The father fell upon his neck and smothered him with kisses. Then he said to the servants, "Bring forth the best robe."

All the time the prodigal is repeating to himself, "Make me a hired servant," his father is saying, "Bring forth the best robe." Servants don't wear robes. "Put a ring on his hand." Servants don't have rings on their fingers. "Put shoes on his feet." Servants don't wear shoes. "Kill the fatted calf." Nobody ever killed a fatted calf for a servant. And the father called him "my son."

The airline calls him a *passenger*,
The doctor calls him a *patient*,

> The lawyer calls him a *client*,
> The grocery man calls him a *customer*,
> The banker calls him a *depositor*,
> The policeman calls him a *renegade*,
> The jailer calls him a *prisoner*,
> But Daddy calls him a *son*.

"For this my son was dead, and is alive again; he was lost, and is found. . . . Bring hither the fatted calf." It was a happy time. His boy is back home!

The prodigal was in his right mind. And about the time he got through part of his speech, "Father, I have sinned against, I have sinned against heaven, and I . . .," his daddy stopped him: "Bring forth. . . ." The son never got to finish his little speech and beg, "Make me a hired servant." He's a son in the house of his daddy.

The most insane people are the Devil's crowd, while the most sensible people are Christians. They are looking at the right thing, for the right reason, at the right time, and God smiles from Heaven and calls them "My children"!

II. WHAT DID NEBUCHADNEZZAR DO?

When in his right mind, he made an about-face—became a totally new person. A total change came over him. All of his bewilderments became blessings. All of his frustrations were resolved. All of his fears were allayed. All of his lost senses now are back. Once again he had self-esteem. But now the king is in control again. He is a new man. No longer does he crawl around on all fours like a beast.

What does he do?

First, he acknowledges that God alone is to be praised. Look at verse 34 again: ". . . and I blessed the most High, and I praised and honoured him . . . ." God is the only one worthy of our praise.

Second, he acknowledges the eternality of God's kingdom

in verse 34: "...whose dominion is an everlasting dominion, and his kingdom is from generation to generation."

Now Nebuchadnezzar's kingdom lasted from 606 to 562 B.C.; then it all came to a screeching halt. He died. His kingdom waned, and the Assyrians took over.

Wait! The kingdom of God is everlasting. Awhile ago Nebuchadnezzar was saying, "This is my kingdom. And I'm an everlasting king—king of kings, lord of lords." But when he got his mind back, he said, 'God only is to be praised, and His kingdom is forever.' He acknowledged that man is nothing in God's sight.

Look at verse 35: "And all the inhabitants of the earth are reputed as nothing." Nothing. Who are we? Zero outside of Jesus Christ, zero with a rim erased off it. Nothing. But thank God, in Him we are eternally bound for Heaven! We are saved, redeemed, regenerated, pardoned, forgiven, justified; we are sons of God by faith in Jesus Christ. We are somebody in Him only.

Third, Nebuchadnezzar acknowledges that no one can prevent God from exercising His will. You remember Jesus taught us to pray, "Thy will be done on earth as it is in heaven." Look with me at verse 35: "...he [God] doeth according to his will in the army of heaven...." You didn't know Heaven had an army? One day when Jesus returns to establish His kingdom on earth, He will come on a white horse, and the armies of Heaven will follow Him. We will be coming 'round the mountain when we come! And riding white horses when we come. Remember that old song? "...and he doeth according to his will in the army of heaven, and among the inhabitants of the earth: and none can stay his hand, or say unto him, What doest thou?"

To ask God, "What are You doing?" is like an axe turning around to the man swinging it and saying, "What are you doing?" He is the Creator. You and I are God's creatures. We have no reason to ask, "God, what are You doing?" Paul puts it so wonderfully in Romans 11:34–36, "For who hath known the mind of the Lord? or who hath been his counsellor? Or who hath first given to him, and it shall be recompensed unto him again? For of him, and through him, and to him, are all things."

You don't tell God what to do, and you don't ask Him what He is doing. "O the depth of the riches both of the wisdom and knowledge of God! how unsearchable are his judgments, and his ways past finding out!"

Don't ever ask, "Can God?" for that is like saying God can't. Don't ever ask, "God, what are You doing to me?" This body belongs to Him; so He is doing what He is doing to His body. Do your children belong to Him? Then He is doing it to His children. Does your business belong to Him? Then He is doing it to His business. Don't ever ask, "God, what are You doing?" He is working out a plan, a pattern. Underneath are ragged edges. We don't always see the beauty, the glory, the majesty of it; but one day we will see it from the top side, see the finished product.

Through sickness and sorrow, through tragedy and loss, through disappointment, discouragement and disillusionment, through all of our ups and downs and ins and outs, God is doing something. So don't ever question God.

Fourth, Nebuchadnezzar acknowledges that God is true and just. Verse 37 reads, "Now I, Nebuchadnezzar, praise and extol and honour the king of heaven, all whose works are truth, and his ways judgment [or just, equitable, fair, honorable, true, honest. He acknowledges that God can bring down those who exalt themselves in private]: and those that walk in pride he is able to abase."

Luke 18:14 tells us, ". . . for every one that exalteth himself shall be abased; and he that humbleth himself shall be exalted."

Proverbs 16:18 warns, "Pride goeth before destruction, and an haughty spirit before a fall."

And I read in I Peter 5:5, "For God resisteth the proud, and giveth grace to the humble."

God will have nothing to do with the proud. Look at Hebrews 11, His Honor Roll. Murderers, liars, whoremongers, adulterers—all kinds of people are listed there. But one man is significantly missing. He is conspicuous by his absence. Saul, first king of Israel, stood head and shoulders above all the others. But in God's Honor Roll we don't find him listed. David, a murderer and an adulterer, is there. And listed are some sorry lots in life; but we don't find Saul. Why? Because he was *proud.* "God resisteth the proud." And, as though we couldn't get it the first time, James turns right around and in James 4:6 says precisely the same thing that Peter said: "God resisteth the proud, and giveth grace unto the humble."

God did something wonderful for Nebuchadnezzar. What He did even improved his looks. We read in verse 36, ". . . brightness returned unto me . . . ." He had already said that his mind came back, so he is not here talking about his mind but about his countenance. He looked better when he got his right mind back because he got right with God.

People always look better when they get right with God. If you go around looking like a sour puss, then we know something is wrong. If you go around griping, complaining, criticizing and flying off the handle, something is wrong.

Nebuchadnezzar looked better; he had a better image.

Not only that, but it enhanced his position. In verse 36 the king said that, when his brightness returned, and his mind and reasoning, even "my counsellors and my lords sought unto me [came again for his advice, counsel and understanding]; and I was established in my kingdom, and excellent majesty was added unto me."

This happened when he got his mind back and when he got back to God.

Getting right with God is the best thing anyone can do. The best thing you can do is come to this altar and get your heart and life right with God. You may be saved already, but something is troubling you and taking away your testimony. It may be some habit, an attitude, your disposition. Something is hurting your testimony. Lay it all on the altar.

III. HOW DID NEBUCHADNEZZAR'S BEHAVIOR AFFECT OTHERS?

Once he got his mind back, the people reestablished their relationship with him. Nobody wants to keep company with a complainer, a backslider, a griper, someone who is out of his mind. When we get in that shape spiritually, we are more or less out of our spiritual minds. Our state of mind and status in life will affect all around us. Daddy, you can't be an old grouch, kick the door down at home, swear and curse and not affect your children. Everything we do affects somebody for eternity.

Paul says in Romans 14:7, "For none of us liveth to himself, and no man dieth to himself." When you do wrong, it affects others. When you do right, it affects others. When you lie down on the job and don't do your part; when you come in late; when you kill time; when you shirk your duty and somebody else has to do it, it affects everybody on the job.

When you and I serve God, we influence others. When we witness for Christ, we influence others to witness. When we give, we influence others to give. When we sing, we influence others to sing. When we pray, we influence others to pray. When we attend church, we influence others to attend. When we do right, we influence others to do right. And when we gripe and complain and bicker and get sour on the world, others will follow us.

The bottom line is: when we are where we ought to be with

God, it causes others to want to be where we are.

I ask you heart to heart, Where are you with God? Does Christ mean anything to you? Does He mean everything to you? On a scale of one to ten, where do you stand with Him?

How many times in these thirty years have people come to my office and said, "Pastor, something is wrong with me spiritually. I don't have any really bad habits, but something is missing."

I take out a pencil and a piece of paper and write down five cylinders every Christian ought to be hitting on: prayer, Bible study, stewardship, witnessing and attending church.

I say, "Now, are you praying like you ought to pray?"

"Well, pastor, you know. . . ." One cylinder already missing.

"Are you reading the Bible?"

"Well, preacher, I have such a busy schedule."

"Are you attending church regularly?"

"Well, I come when I—you know how it is, preacher."

"Are you giving?"

"Well, now let me tell you, preacher. I can't afford. . . ."

"Are you witnessing?"

Then I go back over the cylinders.

"Okay. You are hitting on only three cylinders. You are missing two."

Go out and crank up your car. Let's say it has eight cylinders. You go out and unplug two, and how far will you get? Gas tank full, tires full of air, nothing wrong with the battery; horn blows, lights burn—but you are missing two or three cylinders. "Chuk-a-chuk-a-chuk-a-chuk-a-chuk-a"—you know how it sounds, and you will not get very far.

No matter who you are nor how long you have been saved nor how long you have been a member of the church, if you have one cylinder missing, power is gone out of your life.

Where do you stand with God? Are you hittin' on all cylinders? If you will be honest with yourself, grade yourself on a scale of one to ten, where would you stand with God?

Now I invite you to come to this altar and tell God you are missing some cylinders, if things aren't exactly like they ought to be. Come if you want to build a better relationship with God or if you want to be a ten for Christ.

In your right mind, you will become a different person.

——— *Outline* 5:5-17 ———

An Unwelcomed Party Pooper

Introduction

The city of Babylon—the **"party-going"** capital of ancient world

Observe this city on the bank of the Euphrates River:

- It was the **pride** of antiquity.
- It was the **kingdom** of all kingdoms.
- It was the **empire** of all empires.
- It was the **excellency** of the Chaldeans.
- Herodotus called it **"The City of Gold."**

In the midst of city of greed, ghouls and gold, Belshazzar reigned supremely—a proud, profane, profligate king.

- He felt safe and secure in his revelry; but before night ended, his sins were written on wall of palace by the finger of God.
- Before carefree celebration was over, he called for a preacher.
- Proverbs 21:1—*"The king's heart. . . ."*

Look again at Babylon:

- It was no average city.
- It was a city of art and architecture.
- It was 15 miles square.
- Its outer walls were 350 feet high.
  - —They were 750 feet thick at the base.
  - —They were 300 feet thick at the top.
  - —Six chariots could roll abreast on top of these massive walls.

- Its inner walls were 250 feet high.
  [On top of this wall a standing army poised to pour pots of hot molten lead on any invading army.]
- In the Chapel of Baal stood 40-foot solid gold statue of Baal [cost: $17 million dollars].

The "Palace of Belshazzar"—city's main attraction
- Dining room: 1650 feet wide/a mile long
- 4,500 pillars shaped like elephants made up the walls.
- The central table in shape of horseshoe and accommodated a thousand lords and ladies.
- Trained peacocks with gold harnesses pulled miniature chariots loaded with wines and meats.
- Outside in the garden an orchestra of 32,000 musicians provided music.

  —What a night!
  —What a celebration event!
  —What a city!

But wait, in the midst of all the dancing, dining and degradation appeared an uninvited, unwelcomed guest.

Message

I. DESECRATION OF THE HOLY

Observe three sins—verses 1–4

A. Sin of **intemperance**: "strong drink"
  - This is a sin against **one's self**.
  - Warning: Proverbs 20:1
    Proverbs 23:29-32
  - 50,000 deaths annually: alcohol related
  - Poisons the mind, the body, and the soul
  - Probably nation's number one drug abuse

B. Sin of **immorality**: "unmentionable vice"
  - This is a sin against **one's fellowman**.

- Look at verse 2: immoral behavior.

C. Sin of **infidelity**: "desecration of the holy"
  - This is a sin against **God**.
  - That which has been sanctified as a vessel unto God must never be desecrated by man.
  - Babylonian party-goers insulted God of Israel / God of Daniel.

  [That is what sin is—an insult to God.]

REMINDER: Your body is the temple of God, a holy vessel (I Cor. 6:19, 20).

WARNING: Don't desecrate vessels of God!

II. HANDWRITING ON THE WALL

OBSERVE: When party is at its most celebrated moment, the "party pooper" enters—verse 5.

A. The fingers of a man's hand—verse 5
  1. The finger was the "finger of God."
  2. The finger wrote a message of doom.
  3. The finger frightened the king beyond measure—verse 6.
     - His countenance changed.
     - His thoughts troubled him.
     - His loins loosened.
     - His knees knocked.

B. The failure of the wise men—verses 7–9

III. INTRODUCTION OF A PROPHET

CONSIDER: Verses 10–16

A. The prophet is a **man** of God.

B. The prophet has the **Spirit** of God—verse 11.
C. The prophet has the **wisdom** of God—verses 11, 12.
   1. Wisdom to interpret dreams
   2. Wisdom to reveal secrets
   3. Wisdom to dissolve doubts

Listen to the king's conversation with Daniel—verse 16.
- "I have heard of you!"
- "I understand you are very wise!"
- "If you interpret the handwriting, I will promote you to a position of great power and prominence."

Observe Daniel's response—verse 17.
- "Keep your gold."
- "Give your rewards to someone else."
- "I'll tell you what God said, and it won't cost you a penny.'

NOTE: Application:
   1. The Christian and the glitter of the world
   2. The Christian as a holy vessel
   3. The Christian and godly living

Conclusion

No Christian can indulge in worldly pursuits and be effective in God's service.

Appeal: Surrender your life to God at the altar of prayer.

CHAPTER TEN

An Unwelcomed Party Pooper

5. *In the same hour came forth fingers of a man's hand, and wrote over against the candlestick upon the plaister of the wall of the king's palace: and the king saw the part of the hand that wrote.*—Dan. 5:5.

Not only in the life of our nation but in the lives of many individuals, the handwriting is on the wall. God is trying to tell America something. Through circumstances, problems, difficulties, trials and out of His blessed Word, God is saying something to us. Are we listening?

Let's go to the city of Babylon, on the banks of the Euphrates River. You heard much about that during Desert Storm. Located about fifty miles south of what is now Baghdad, Iraq, was the ancient Babylon, the "party-going" capital of the ancient world. In the city of Babylon were the Hanging Gardens, built by Nebuchadnezzar for one of his wives. It was the pride of antiquity.

Babylon was the kingdom of all kingdoms, the empire of all empires. It was the excellency of the Chaldeans' glory. Herodotus, Greek historian, called it the "city of gold."

In the midst of that city of greed, ghouls and gold, Belshazzar reigned supremely. A proud, profane, profligate king was he. You would have to travel a long way to find one more debauched, more degraded, than this grandson of Nebuchadnezzar.

Look at verse 5: "In the same hour. . . ." God knows just *when* to do what He does. Nobody has to punch the clock for God, nobody has to wake Him up in the morning; for "He that keepeth Israel shall neither slumber nor sleep."

"In the same hour. . . ." Belshazzar felt very secure in his revelry; but before the night was over, he would see his own sins written by the fingers of God on the walls of his own palace. Before this great carefree celebration was over, he would call for a preacher. Proverbs 21:1 reminds us, "The king's heart is in the hand of the Lord, as the rivers of water: he turneth it whithersoever he will."

Look again at Babylon. It was no average city. It was a city of art and architecture, a city of books and brains, of living and learning, of lust and licentiousness. It was a city of degradation and debauchery. The outer walls of the fifteen-mile-square Babylon were 350 feet high; at the base, 750 feet thick. At the top they were 300 feet wide, which meant six chariots could roll abreast on top of the walls of the ancient Babylon. The inner walls were 250 feet high, and on top a garrison of soldiers were ready to pour hot molten lead upon the heads of the invading armies.

That statue would cost 17 million dollars; and the military budget, a billion dollars a year in our currency—quite a city, quite an army.

It was a city of worship, but a worship of pagan gods.

The chief attraction, however, was the palace of Belshazzar, in the central part of the city. The dining room was no average dining room—1650 feet wide and one mile long. The central table could accommodate a thousand lords, their wives and concubines. Trained peacocks with gold harnesses pulled many a golden cart up and down the table loaded with wines and meats for Belshazzar, his thousand lords, their wives and concubines.

In the garden an orchestra of 32,000 players furnished the music. What a night! What a celebration! What a city!

But in the midst of all the dancing, dining and degradation appeared an uninvited and unwelcomed guest, the party pooper. Sometimes God comes on the scene when we're having our little party and breaks in, uninvited, unannounced and unwelcomed. Such was the case here. "In the same hour . . . ," with all the revelry, rejoicing, drinking, dining, dancing—with all of the celebration, "came forth fingers of a man's hand [in the palace of Belshazzar] and wrote . . . and the king saw the part of the hand that wrote."

I will talk about this "unwelcomed party pooper" and three things that happened.

I. DESECRATION OF THE HOLY

Observe out of verses 1 through 4 three notable sins.

1. *Belshazzar the king made a great feast to a thousand of his lords, and drank wine before the thousand.*

With a few drinks under his belt, a fellow really thinks he's somebody. Young men, don't pattern your life after him, but pattern it after someone sober. Drinkers do stupid things, wild things. I know it looks like such a man is a big hero, but he is only a little man who intoxicates his mind and body with strong drink. The Bible calls him foolish.

2. *Belshazzar, whiles he tasted the wine, commanded to bring the golden and silver vessels which his father* [literally his grand-father] *Nebuchadnezzar had taken out of the temple which was in Jerusalem; that the king, and his princes, his wives, and his concubines, might drink therein.*

3. *Then they brought the golden vessels that were taken out*

of the temple [these vessels came from the house of God] *of the house of God which was at Jerusalem; and the king, and his princes, his wives, and his concubines, drank in them.*

4. *They drank wine, and praised the gods of gold, and of silver, of brass, of iron, of wood, and of stone.*

The desecration of the holy.

There are three notable sins.

First, the sin of *intemperance*—strong drink. This sin man commits against himself. Proverbs 20:1 warns, "Wine is a mocker, strong drink is raging: and whosoever is deceived thereby is not wise."

A longer passage on drink is in Proverbs 23:29–35:

Who hath woe? who hath sorrow? who hath contentions? who hath babbling? who hath wounds without cause? who hath redness of eyes? They that tarry long at the wine; they that go to seek mixed wine. Look not thou upon the wine when it is red, when it giveth his colour in the cup, when it moveth itself aright. At the last it biteth like a serpent, and stingeth like an adder. Thine eyes shall behold strange women, and thine heart shall utter perverse things. Yea, thou shalt be as he that lieth down in the midst of the sea, or as he that lieth upon the top of a mast. They have stricken me, shalt thou say, and I was not sick; they have beaten me, and I felt it not: when shall I awake? I will seek it yet again.

A man can't take just one drink and be satisfied. He goes back after it again. Fifty thousand deaths annually in America are attributed to alcohol. It poisons mind, body and soul. Probably the nation's number one drug abuse is alcohol. When parents try to get their children not to take drugs, but let them go on guzzling Coors, they don't make sense.

Second, the sin of *immorality*—unmentionable vice. This is a sin against man's fellowman. How many homes are broken because of immoral behavior! Daniel 5:2 gives a description about wine, the king, his princes, his wives, his concubines. Can you imagine the debauchery, the immoral behavior that went on in that palace that night?

Third, the sin of *infidelity*—the desecration of the holy vessels of God. With the sin of intemperance—strong drink—man sins against himself. With the sin of immorality—unmentionable vices—men sin against others. But the sin of infidelity is the sin against God.

We have no right to desecrate a vessel that God has declared holy and has sanctified for His own use. Out of the Temple at Jerusalem, the house of God, the house of prayer, came these golden vessels and the desecration of the vessels by those who would pour wine into these holy items. These Babylonian party-goers insulted God Himself.

What is sin but an insult to God? When we do any sin, we insult Him. I remind you that your body is the temple of the Holy Spirit, a holy vessel according to I Corinthians 6:19: "What? know ye not that your body is the temple of the Holy Ghost which is in you, which ye have of God, and ye are not your own? For ye are bought with a price: therefore glorify God in your body, and in your spirit, which are God's."

You may argue, "It's my body; I can do what I want with it." No, you can't. First, it isn't your body if you belong to Christ. When I was sick, I told God, "If You want to have Your body operated on, all right. If You want Your body to be feeble and weak, let it be so," remembering that my body is His body. When we desecrate that body, we desecrate the body of Christ, who is the exalted Head in Heaven; and there will be a reckoning day. The handwriting will come on the wall.

So don't desecrate the holy vessel of God.

II. HANDWRITING ON THE WALL

At the highest moment of celebration, the party pooper enters. "In the same hour . . ."—not next week. You and I don't choose the time for God to come and say, "This is what you ought to be doing." We don't choose the time when God comes and says, "I'm bringing this about in your life for your good." (By the way, Romans 8:28 is still in the Bible: "And we know that all things work together for good to them that love God"— be it loss of health, loss of mind or loss of job.)

When God wants to say something to America, when God wants to say something to Worth Baptist Church, when God wants to say something to you and me, what does He do? In a moment, totally unexpected, He may come on the scene and with His hand write a message of doom. "In the same hour came forth fingers of a man's hand, and wrote over against the candlestick. . . ." Belshazzar saw what looked like a man's hand. Because God can describe Himself only in terms we can understand, we have to know that this was more than the hand of a man. These fingers were the fingers of God.

The finger of God wrote the Ten Commandments.

It was the finger of God that wrote on the ground when the accusers of a fallen woman were ready to stone her—the only time we hear of Him writing in the New Testament. We are not told what He wrote; it may have been the sins of those who had the stones in their hands. Then He said to them, "He that is without sin among you, let him first cast a stone at her." People who live in glass houses ought not throw stones.

We are all sinners. Only by the grace of God are we not staggering down some back alley picking up bottles to sell to get another jug of cheap wine. There is no difference in the sophisticated sinner who sits in the pew and the sinner out there pushing the cart and picking up bottles to get another jug of wine. None whatsoever.

We try to sophisticate our sins. Probably none of you would be caught picking up bottles by the curb to sell to get another drink. But what about those sophisticated sins such as robbing God, failure to read your Bible and failure to win souls? "To him that knoweth to do good, and doeth it not, to him it is sin."

The fingers of God wrote. The message of doom came. It frightened the king beyond measure:

6. *Then the king's countenance was changed* [a different look came over his face], *and his thoughts troubled him, so that the joints of his loins were loosed, and his knees smote one against another.*

You've often wondered where that old saying came from, "I was so scared my knees were knocking." Now you know.

Handwriting on the wall. Fingers of God. Fear in the king's heart.

The wise men, who thought they knew it all, failed the test miserably. Verses 7 through 9 say:

7. *The king cried aloud to bring in the astrologers, the Chaldeans, and the soothsayers. And the king spake, and said to the wise men of Babylon, Whosoever shall read this writing, and shew me the interpretation thereof, shall be clothed with scarlet, and have a chain of gold about his neck, and shall be the third ruler in the kingdom.*

8. *Then came in all the king's wise men: but they could not read the writing, nor make known to the king the interpretation thereof.*

9. *Then was king Belshazzar greatly troubled, and his countenance was changed in him, and his lords were astonied.*

The unsaved cannot understand the Bible because it is spiritually discerned. It takes the Holy Spirit to interpret this Book. The unsaved can't read the writing of God. Wise men failed to do it.

Ladies and gentlemen, the wisdom of this world is not enough to get you to God. All our degrees, all our education, all our learning won't get us to Heaven. Men don't go to Heaven by educational degrees. I'm not against education, but too many are depending on what they know, who they are and where they have been. The wisdom of this world is foolishness in God's sight. "Because the foolishness of God is wiser than men; and the weakness of God is stronger than men," says the Bible. No man can take an examination and pass it to get to Heaven. He has to go by way of the cross.

> **I must needs go home by the way of the cross,**
> **There's no other way but this;**
> **I shall ne'er get sight of the Gates of Light,**
> **If the way of the cross I miss.**

Wisdom from below is earthly, sensual, devilish. You can't educate men into Heaven; you can't philosophize men into Heaven. Men go to Heaven by way of Jesus. They go through the blood and only through the blood.

III. INTRODUCTION OF A PROPHET

10. *Now the queen by reason of the words of the king and his lords came into the banquet house. . . and said, O king, live for ever: let not thy thoughts trouble thee, nor let thy countenance be changed:*

11. *There is a man in thy kingdom, in whom is the spirit of the holy gods. . . .*

The queen knew something was different about Daniel. She wasn't versed enough in theology to say it was the Holy Spirit of God, but she recognized there was a different Spirit.

The born-again believer has a different Spirit from the world. When what is on the *inside* is different, it is reflected by what is on the *outside*—by the way we dress, by the way we talk, by the way we walk. Dr. J. Frank Norris used to say, "When I see something that waddles like a duck, and quacks like a duck, and swims like a duck, I call it a duck." If it's on the inside, it will show up on the outside—where we go, what we do and with whom we do it, the books we read and the movies we watch. We sit around and curse Hollywood; yet we bring it right into our front room and let our children watch it on video or put them to bed, and we watch it after they've gone to sleep. And that is wrong!

Let me compliment one of our little fellows, Matthew Carter. His daddy said to me, "He's in a little business of his own. He's picking up cans off the street."

I asked, "Does he pick up Coors?"

"No, not Coors. He doesn't want to pick up the Devil's cans."

If a little fellow doesn't want to touch it, we grown folks certainly ought not want to touch it. Don't draw a line. No double standard.

The handwriting is on the wall for America, for religious America, for church-going America. I say it one more time: When the Holy Spirit of God is on the *inside,* it will show on the *outside.*

Here is Daniel, a prophet of God who had the Spirit of God and the wisdom of God to interpret dreams.

12. . . . *an excellent spirit, and knowledge, and understanding, interpreting of dreams, and shewing of hard sentences, and dissolving of doubts, were found in the same Daniel. . . let Daniel be called, and he will shew the interpretation.*

It's so good to see a person with an excellent spirit, one who is not always griping, complaining and bickering.

I know some who suffer bodily, but they have an excellent spirit. I know some who couldn't buy you a hamburger, but they have an excellent spirit. It doesn't take money nor the upper echelon to have an excellent spirit. You don't have to be among the upper crust (a few crumbs held together by a little dough!). It doesn't take money, fame, popularity, a good standing in society to have an excellent spirit. The Spirit of God is the giver.

The king said to Daniel, this man with excellent wisdom,

knowledge and understanding, this man who can interpret dreams, reveal dark secrets and dissolve all doubts:

16. *And I have heard of thee, that thou canst make interpretations, and dissolve doubts. . . .*

How would you like to have someone around who could dissolve your doubts? You do have—the Holy Spirit.

The king said, "I have heard of thee. . . ." When we are living for Jesus and walking with Jesus and have a good spirit, people will hear about it. "I've heard of you. I've heard how faithful you are to your church. I've heard what a good witness you are for Jesus, how you read your Bible and are regular at Sunday school, how you sing in the choir and live as you ought to live, and how on the job you act as you ought to act. I've heard about you."

"*. . . now if thou canst read the writing, and make known to me the interpretation thereof, thou shalt be clothed with scarlet, and have a chain of gold about thy neck, and shalt be the third ruler in the kingdom.*"

Those were Belshazzar's words to Daniel. Listen to Daniel's answer:

17. *Let thy gifts be to thyself, and give thy rewards to another; yet I will read the writing unto the king, and make known to him the interpretation.*

In other words, "Keep your gold. Give your gifts to somebody else. Reading the writing won't cost you a penny."

Tonight God is offering you the best He has. He has paid it all—paid everything.

> **Jesus paid it all,**
> **All to Him I owe;**
> **Sin had left a crimson stain,**
> **He washed it white as snow.**

Come, buy without money and without price. Ho, everyone

that thirsteth, come. It won't cost you a penny. Jesus has already taken care of the debt. The old account was settled long ago.

Daniel told the king, "Keep your gold. Give your gifts to another. I'll read the writing for you without a penny."

Let us make an application in our own individual lives. Every person is an individual; no two are alike. What might affect you might not have any effect on somebody else. But God's Word speaks to us all in one way or another. Christian, don't be carried away with the glitter of gold, the dollars and cents. There is nothing wrong with having things, but it's when things have you that the problem comes.

The Christian and the holy vessel: Don't desecrate the holy temple of God Almighty.

The Christian and godly living:

**So live, that when thy summons comes to join
The innumerable caravan, which moves
To that mysterious realm, where each shall take
His chamber in the silent halls of death,
Thou go not, like the quarry-slave at night,
Scourged to his dungeon, but, sustained and soothed
By an unfaltering trust, approach thy grave,
Like one who wraps the drapery of his couch
About him, and lies down to pleasant dreams.**
—William Cullen Bryant

Be ready to die.

Godly living: "For the grace of God that bringeth salvation hath appeared to all men, Teaching us that, denying ungodliness and worldly lusts, we should live soberly, righteously, and godly, in this present world."

No Christian can indulge in worldly pursuits, then be effective in God's service. Surrender your life to God tonight at the altar of prayer. You have seen the handwriting on the wall of your own heart. God has spoken to you; and if you want the Lord God to be the Lord, Master Governor, Guide and Guardian of your life, He wants to be and will be if you will let Him in.

You remember that famous painting, "The Light of the World," done by Holman Hunt. Hunt has depicted Christ standing at a door, firmly shut, in the half light of the evening, with His right hand upon the knocker. At His feet, weeds have grown tall, for the door had not been opened for many a year. Thus, Christ stands patiently awaiting a response—His head haloed, His kingly crown entwined with the crown of thorns, in His left hand a lantern, casting a flickering light upon the weeds entwining the door, and showing us the nail prints in His pierced hands.

When the picture was first exhibited in London, critics immediately said that Hunt had made an omission. On the door there is a knocker, but there is no outside handle. Hunt had his reply: "This door opens only from the inside."

Yes, it is the door of a man's heart, and it opens only to those who open it. If any man hear and open the door, Christ will come in.

A Kingdom Comes Crashing Down

Introduction

- Unusual events in Babylon
- "Kingdom by the river" is troubled.
- God has intervened in affairs of men.
- A divine demonstration has taken place.
- Nothing will ever be the same.

[I think I should tell you that, when God intervenes in your life, you will never be the same.]

Message

I. A REVIEW OF HISTORY—verses 18–21
   READ: Verses 18–21
   Notice three things about Nebuchadnezzar:
   A. His exaltation—verse 18
   B. His adoration—verse 19
   C. His humiliation—verses 20, 21

NOTE: From his pedestal of pride, he came down to platform humiliation.
—From palace to a pallet
—From plenty to poverty
—From a potentate to a pauper
(From riches to rags, and from prominence, position and power to zero)

II. A POWERFUL INDICTMENT
    READ: Verses 22, 23

Observe three things about Belshazzar in this indictment:

A. His refusal to humble himself—verse 22
(This, in spite of his knowledge of history of his grandfather)

B. His desecration of holy vessels—verse 23

C. His failure to glorify God—verse 23

III. A COLOSSAL COLLAPSE

READ: Verses 24–30

A. The king weighed—verse 27

NOTE: On the way to eternity every man steps onto scales of Almighty God.
1. There is no discrepancy in God's assessment of mankind.
(The divine scales are always right.)
2. There is no rebuttal of God's decision.
3. There is no appeal to a higher authority.
   • God **knows** all things.
   • God **sees** all things.
   • God **controls** all things.
   • God **judges** all things.
   • God is **above** all, **over** all and **beyond** all.

B. The divine verdict—verse 27
Consider God's disposal of His enemies:

• Pharaoh will blaspheme God's name, but the waters of the Red Sea will swallow him alive.

• Jezebel will swear against God's prophet, but the dogs will lick up her blood.

• Herod will cast Peter and James into prison, but worms will devour his flesh while he sits on his throne.

> **NOTE:** Time after time men have opposed God, but the verdict has always been the same: **"FOUND WANTING!"**

- **MENE**—"The days of your life are numbered" (finished).
- **TEKEL**—"Thou art weighed. . . found wanting" (come up short).
- **PERES**—"Thy kingdom is divided" (power diminished).
  —the Pharaohs
  —the Nebuchadnezzars
  —the Tiglath-Pilezers
  —the Sargons
  —the Shalmanesers
  —the Belshazzars
  —the Caesars
  —the Napoleons
  —the Hitlers
  —the Stalins
  . . . All discovered the horror of falling into the hands of an angry God!

Read: Verse 30
Observe the divine commentary: *"In that night was Belshazzar the King of the Chaldeans slain."*

- The night of **revelry** became a night of **ruin**.
- The night of **celebration** became a night of **consternation**.
- The night of **debauchery** became a night of **death**. (The king had no thought of dying.)

QUESTION: What about you?
  —You have no thought of dying.

—You plan the greatest celebration of your life.

—You expect to live a long time.

ILLUSTRATION: "The rich fool" (Luke 16)

WARNING: Hebrews 9:27

REMINDER: This is no time for the preacher to mince words.
- The judgment of God must come upon all dis-obedience (Rom. 1:18).
- You can't sin and get by with it (Gal. 6:7).
- Judgment swift and sure (Prov. 29:1).

QUESTION: How much do you weigh on God's scales?

If you do not weigh enough, if you are "weighed and found wanting," I recommend:

1. A proper diet of God's Word.
2. Proper exercise in God's work.
3. Proper communication in prayer.

Poem: "There Will Always Be Our God"

Conclusion

The only escape from the wrath of God is the blood of His Son.

Appeal: Come to Jesus for salvation, safety and security.

CHAPTER ELEVEN

 A Kingdom Comes Crashing Down

30. *In that night was Belshazzar the king of the Chaldeans slain.*

Some unusual events had taken place in the kingdom of Belshazzar; and before him, in the kingdom of his grandfather, Nebuchadnezzar. In the days of these great kings, the kingdom in that land called the land of Mesopotamia, between the Tigris and the Euphrates Rivers, was the city of Babylon, the capital of the Babylonian Empire. We can trace its origin back to the book of Genesis and the tower of Babel, or the tower of confusion. When we go contrary to the way God wants something done, it always results in confusion, whether it be a nation, a church, a family or an individual. Babylon learned her lesson. God had intervened in the affairs of men. He had come on the scene with a divine demonstration that had taken place in the capital city. Nothing after that could ever be the same.

Once you have had a personal confrontation with Jesus Christ, your life can never be the same. When God steps in to judge our lives, they can never be the same. The kingdom of Babylon was never the same after this fateful hour, when the handwriting by the finger of God appeared on the wall of Belshazzar in his great palace.

In my message, "A Kingdom Comes Crashing Down," there are three areas of thought.

I. A REVIEW OF HISTORY

We do well to look back to see what God has done in the lives of some individuals that we know. Certainly no person is here tonight, whatever your status, who hasn't experienced in some way or another the hand of God. Whether you have thought it was good or bad, right or wrong, God has done something in your life.

God is trying to say something to America. We are seeing so much debauchery, sin, degradation, drug trafficking, pornography, homosexuality, and I put apathy among Christians right up there with the rest of them. I've talked to many preachers in the last few days; and almost without exception, everyone has said to me, "In all the years of my pastorate, I have never seen people so apathetic about the work of God."

I ask you tonight, How much do you care if men go to Hell? What did you do last week to keep somebody out of Hell? We can talk about how much we love souls, about how much we want to see them saved and about how much we want to see the work of Christ progress and the church grow and Christians glow; but if we're not doing anything about it, our talk doesn't really mean much.

I too can say that in forty years of ministry and thirty years in one pulpit, I have never seen it when so many people cared so little about so much. Apathy is a sin that can be ranked right up there with these other sins that I have mentioned.

Do we really care? We ought to review history once in awhile to see what God is up to.

18. *O thou king, the most high God gave Nebuchadnezzar thy father* [Actually, it was his grandfather, but generations are often named by one single parenting.] *a kingdom, and majesty, and glory, and honour.*

Now let me stop to observe three things about Nebuchadnezzar out of verses 18 through 21.

Number one—his *exaltation*. God gave him a *kingdom*. (Health, strength, happiness, money, home, car, clothes, mind, family, business, job, shoes—whatever you have God has given it to you.) God gave Nebuchadnezzar a kingdom.

But that is not all He gave him. He gave him *majesty*. But that's not all He gave him. He gave him *glory*. But that's not all He gave him. He gave him *honor*.

God exalted Nebuchadnezzar. He was a pagan king, but God rules in pagan nations like He rules in what we used to be able to call a Christian nation. How can we now characterize the United States of America as a Christian nation? We sing, "God bless America"; but can we expect God to do anything for a nation that is stubborn, rebellious, obstinate, drifting away, backsliding, and making a holiday out of His holy day? How can we expect God to bless America?

But God blessed Nebuchadnezzar, gave him a kingdom, gave him majesty, gave him glory, gave him honor. That is his exaltation.

Number two—his *adoration*. Look how people felt about him:

19. *And for the majesty that he gave him, all people, nations, and languages, trembled and feared before him* [respected him]: *whom he would he slew; and whom he would he kept alive; and whom he would he set up; and whom he would he put down.*

He had a tremendous admiration society. This adoration made him a proud king.

So there follows naturally the third thing—his *humiliation*.

20. *But when his heart was lifted up* [he became proud], *and his mind hardened in pride, he was deposed* [put down, humiliated] *from his kingly throne, and they took his glory from him.*

No longer is he admired, no longer is he adored, no longer

is he held high on a pedestal. He is now dethroned, deposed, degraded, cast out, and his glory is taken from him.

21. *And he was driven from the sons of men; and his heart was made like the beasts, and his dwelling was with the wild asses: they fed him with grass like oxen, and his body was wet with the dew of heaven; till he knew that the most high God ruled in the kingdom of men, and that he* [God] *appointeth over it whomsoever he will.*

He was out in the wild eating grass like an ox. You know from an earlier account that the hair on his body grew like feathers, his fingernails grew like eagle's claws, and for seven years he lived like a beast. This stayed on him *"till he knew"* that God ruled in the kingdom of men and appointed whom He wanted.

There are some things we ought to get settled. God is ruling in the affairs of men. He is ruling nations. God is in control. God has the last word.

God can do anything in your life and mine that He wants to. God can put us up; God can bring us down. God can make us rich; God can make us poor. After all, we are His property, His possession. Since our bodies are temples of His Holy Spirit, He has every right and reason to do whatever He wants to. He can do that to anybody, because every man is accountable to God. We must all appear before the judgment seat of Christ— every man. One day every knee shall bow and every tongue shall confess that Jesus Christ is Lord. God has every right to do whatever He chooses to do. He sets up whom He will; He puts down whom He will.

Observe with me, from that pedestal of pride, how Belshazzar came down to a platform of humiliation. From a palace to a pallet, from plenty to poverty, from a potentate to just a poor, less-than-ordinary man. In fact, the Bible says he was taken away from the sons of men. From riches to rags, from prominence, position and power to zero. That's how quickly God can change a life.

Let us not be heard to boast about who we are or what we can do or how powerful or right or mighty or strong or prominent or positioned we are, because in a flash God can move on the scene, write with His finger and spell our doom. History proves it. We just saw a review of history.

II. A POWERFUL INDICTMENT

22. *And thou his son, O Belshazzar, hast not humbled thine heart, though thou knewest all this;*

23. *But hast lifted up thyself against the Lord of heaven; and they have brought the vessels of his house before thee, and thou, and thy lords, thy wives, and thy concubines, have drunk wine in them; and thou hast praised the gods of silver, and gold, of brass, iron, wood, and stone, which see not, nor hear, nor know: and the God in whose hand thy breath is, and whose are all thy ways, hast thou not glorified.*

That is amazing. People are so stupid that they will worship gods of gold, silver, wood, iron and stone that can't see, hear, save or speak, then fail to give God adoration, worship and praise. How foolish can people be? What an indictment!

God, through the Prophet Daniel, indicts this man Belshazzar with three things.

(1) *His refusal to humble himself before God: "Thou . . . hast not humbled thine heart."* He worshiped gods of gold and silver. He failed to humble himself before God, with a knowledge of what God had already done to his grandfather for doing the same thing.

When are we going to learn? Why can't we look at history and see how God has judged nations and know how He's going to judge the United States of America? The wicked shall be turned into Hell and every nation that forgets God.

Who are we? Oh, we say, "We the people," but you know the Babylonians said the same thing—"We the people." When are we going to learn from what God has already done out of the pages of history, what He is going to do again?

Belshazzar knew exactly what God had done to his grandfather because of his pride, his arrogance, his stubbornness, his rebellion, his obstinacy and his disobedience; yet in spite of his knowledge of that, he did the same thing.

Young people, take a lesson from the generation that has gone before you. You've seen what God has done. When God gives you examples of what another generation has done, for God's sake, learn from that lesson and don't be guilty of the same.

Not only did God indict him because he refused to humble himself, but God indicted him because

(2) *He desecrated holy vessels.* He did the same thing his grandfather did. All of those vessels they had brought out of God's house. Listen! What is in God's house is holy and sacred. Our bodies are holy and sacred because God lives in them. Let us not allow one thing to enter the temple of the Holy Spirit that would desecrate His body. '. . . the vessels that you brought out of the house of God, along with your wives and your concubines, you have drunk wine in; and you have desecrated those vessels.' It is a dangerous thing to desecrate the vessels of a holy God.

(3) *His failure to glorify God.* "Hast thou not glorified" the very God who gave you breath, the very God who controls your life, the very God who puts the sun up there by day and the moon by night, who gives rain and who gives the harvest, the crop, health, strength and all the rest. What an indictment!

Have you humbled yourself before God? Have you given God the glory, the praise, the honor, the credit due Him? Have you been guilty of desecrating the holy vessel, the temple of God? Have you failed to praise and glorify the God of Heaven, the

God of Abraham, of Isaac and Jacob? If so, God is indicting you tonight.

Following the indictment comes

III. A COLOSSAL COLLAPSE

24. *Then was the part of the hand sent from him; and this writing was written.*

It was a gala affair. Babylon was at her best. Crowds had thronged the palace. People were drinking out of the vessels from the house of God and having their good time. All of a sudden God wrote against the wall.

25. *And this is the writing that was written, MENE, MENE, TEKEL, UPHARSIN.*

26. *This is the interpretation of the thing: MENE; God hath numbered thy kingdom, and finished it.* [When God does a thing, He does it well—nothing added to it; nothing taken from it.]

27. *Tekel; Thou art weighed in the balances, and art found wanting.*

28. *Peres; Thy kingdom is divided, and given to the Medes and Persians.*

Then there's a little parenthetical sentence:

29. *. . . and they clothed Daniel with scarlet, and put a chain of gold about his neck, and made a proclamation concerning him, that he should be the third ruler in the kingdom.*

30. *In that night was Belshazzar the king of the Chaldeans slain.*

Let's first look at the king's *weight.* How much did he weigh on God's scales?

On the way to eternity, every man steps on the scales of God. God weighs us against the standard of righteousness and truth. And when we don't come up to what God says in His Word, we have a problem. God begins to deal with us and speak to us. God begins to convince us, to convict us, and show us we have fallen short.

Every man, I repeat, steps on God's scales. You may not want to step on the scales of your neighbor, friend, but you're going to step on God's scales.

My wife was at the doctor's office a few weeks ago. One of the first things they do is weigh you. My wife stepped up, and the scales went beyond 150. She doesn't weigh that much. They kept on going. Finally the nurse put the weight on it, and it went to 165. My wife said, "Now, wait just a minute! There's no way."

The nurse asked, "Have you gained a little?"

"Well, maybe, but I certainly don't weigh 165 pounds."

"These scales are never wrong."

My wife asked, "Do you have another scale anywhere?"

"Yes, we do."

"Let's go try it."

Sure enough, she hadn't gained weight.

My wife burst out laughing. The nurse said to her, "What on earth is so funny about this?"

"I'm just thinking about all those women you've sent home on a starvation diet who think they weigh 150 or 165 or 170 pounds!"

It will never happen that way on God's scales. They are always accurate. They will measure you for what you really are—no discrepancy. There's no rebuttal; you can't argue with God. There's no appeal higher than His authority. For these gods spoken of in Daniel 5, gods of gold, silver, stone, iron and wood cannot see, cannot speak and cannot save.

I've come to tell you that God knows all things, sees all things, controls all things, judges all things, possesses all things, and is above all things, beyond all things and over all things.

How much do you weigh on God's scales?

Let's be a little more specific. In the reading of God's Word, how much do you weigh?

How much do you weigh in soul winning? When was the last time you witnessed to somebody and said, "Look, I want to see you saved. I'm praying for you"?

How much do you weigh on the financial scale? How far are you behind in your tithes? It's time we got down to business with God.

God is weighing you financially. God is weighing you morally. God is weighing you scripturally. God is weighing you in your witnessing and soul-winning program. How much do you weigh on His scales?

Look at the verdict in verse 27: *"Thou art weighed in the balances, and art found wanting."* God always deals fairly. Pharaoh will blaspheme God's name, but the waters of the Red Sea will swallow him alive. Jezebel will swear against God's prophet, but the dogs will lick up her blood. Herod will put James and Peter in prison, but the worms will eat him alive while he's on his throne giving a great oration. Time after time men have opposed God; the verdict has always been the same: *Found wanting.*

The days of your life are numbered. You are weighed and found wanting. You come up short.

God says, "Thy kingdom is divided," your power is diminished. All the Pharaohs, all the Nebuchadnezzars, all the Tiglath-pilesers, all the Shalmanesers, all the Sargons, all the Caesars, all the Napoleons, all the Hitlers, all the Stalins—all have discovered what it is to fall into the hands of an angry God. You may not mean business with God, but God means business. He is weighing you and me.

Look at that divine commentary again in verse 30, simply, sublimely and very briefly stated: "In that night was Belshazzar the king of the Chaldeans slain." The night of revelry had become a night of ruin. The night of celebration had become a night of consternation. The night of debauchery had become a night of death. The king had had no thought of dying. Why, he was having the best time of his life. He planned the greatest celebration of his entire lifetime.

Neither do you have any thought of dying. I rather doubt that today any of us have said, "Well, I might die today. I wonder what's going to happen." We had better begin to think about it, because "it is appointed unto men once to die."

The rich fool in the New Testament had no thought of dying. He said, "I've got plenty. I'll build bigger barns and tear down these old ones. I'll store up many goods, much fruits, much food. I have a long time to live, so I'm going to enjoy it." It's dangerous to remember the gift but forget who gave it to us. How many times he said *I* and *my*! "*I* will," "*my* barns," "*my* soul." "*I* will say to *my* soul, Soul, take it easy. You've got many days to live."

But like a bolt of lightning out of the sky there came that night these words from God, "Thou fool, this night thy soul shall be required of thee: then whose shall those things be, which thou hast provided?"

You are storing up for a long time to live. I hope you do live long, but you have no guarantee. You're probably not thinking about dying, but death is coming. Both the king and the rich fool thought they were going to live. But listen! The judgment of God must come upon all disobedience. Since He is a righteous God, His very nature demands that sin be punished. "For the wrath of God is revealed from heaven against all ungodliness and unrighteousness of men" (Rom. 1:18). It has to come.

And the judgment of God is sure and steadfast. Proverbs 29:1 warns, "He, that being often reproved hardeneth his neck, shall suddenly be destroyed, and that without remedy." God cannot allow sin to go unpunished. Paul says in Galatians 6, "Be not deceived; God is not mocked: for whatsoever a man soweth, that shall he also reap. For he that soweth to his flesh shall of the flesh reap corruption; but he that soweth to the Spirit shall of the Spirit reap life everlasting."

How are you coming along? How much do you weigh on God's scales? If you are found wanting, let me suggest the proper diet of the Word of God. Let me suggest a proper exercise in the ministry of the church. Let me suggest a proper communication in prayer.

Men have lifted up their fists and power against God, and God sits in Heaven and laughs at them. Out of the pages of history come these words:

THERE WILL ALWAYS BE A GOD

They cannot shell His temple,
Nor dynamite His throne;
They cannot bomb His city,
Nor rob Him of His own.
They cannot take Him captive,
Nor strike Him deaf nor blind,
Nor starve Him to surrender,
Nor make Him change His mind.
They cannot cause Him panic,
Nor cut off His supplies;
They cannot take His kingdom,
Nor hurt Him with their lies.
Though all the world be shattered,
His truth remains the same,
His righteous laws still potent,
And God is still His name.
Though we face war and struggle,
And feel their goad and rod,
We know above confusion,
There will always be our God.

―――― *Outline* 6:1–23 ――――

Lions With Lockjaw

Introduction

What a Man Is Daniel!

- His biography makes for interesting reading.
- Who can compare to this fearless, forceful, faithful servant of God?
- Who among all the prophets has such stamina, steadfastness, and solidarity?
- What other man in the Bible displayed such courage, convictions, character as this death-defying, devil-disturbing hero of the faith?
- We can easily detect the **"iron strand"** in him as we consider odds up against which he went in the pompous palace of a pagan potentate.

Message

I. DANIEL'S EXALTED POSITION

READ: Verses 1, 2

  A. **Perimeters** of kingdom—verse 1
1. 626–536 B.C.—Babylon ruled the world.
2. Nebuchadnezzar and Belshazzar
3. 536–331 B.C.—Medes and Persians
4. Darius, the Mede—536–530 B.C.
5. Cyrus, the Persian—536–530 B.C.
6. 120 provinces: India to Ethiopia
(Babylonian system forming now)

B. **Prominence** of Daniel—verse 2
   1. Three presidents
   2. Daniel was first.
   3. From "retirement" to "royalty"
      • From death of Nebuchadnezzar (562 B.C.) until destruction of Babylon (536 B.C.). Daniel was demoted to an inferior position in retirement (demoted by Evil-merodach).
      • God brings men on the scene that the times demand.
        —For every Pharaoh there's a Moses.
        —For every Herod, a John the Baptist.
        —For every Nero, a Paul.
      • In this generation, God has raised up some men to defy the Devil, denounce sin, and declare the Gospel.
      • Thank God for men of courage, conviction, and character!

II. DANIEL'S EXCELLENT SPIRIT

READ: Verse 3

A. **Preferred** by the king—verse 3a
B. **Possessed** by the Spirit—verse 3b

OBSERVATION: Three things give evidence of the Spirit in Daniel.
   1. Self-control
      • Controlled his physical appetite—1:8
      • Crucified flesh—Galatians 2:20
      • Denied ungodliness and worldly lusts
      • Titus 2:11–13—*"The grace of God...."*
   2. Genuine holiness—Hebrews 12:14
   3. Unwavering faith—II Timothy 4:7

III. DANIEL'S EXCEPTIONAL BEHAVIOR

READ: Verses 4, 5

A. **Faithful** in his belief—verse 4a
B. **Faultless** in his behavior—verse 4b
C. **Firm** in the Book—verse 5
  - Psalm 119:11—*"Thy word...."*
  - Jeremiah 15:16—*"Thy words were found...."*
  - Joshua 1:8—*"This book of the law...."*
  - II Timothy 2:15—*"Study to shew...."*

IV. DANIEL'S EFFECTUAL PRAYER

READ: Verse 10; James 5:16

OBSERVATION: reminder of king's decree—verse 7
"No prayer for thirty days"

A. **Danger** he encountered—verse 7
B. **Discipline** he exhibited—verse 10

[I think I should tell you: God does not keep office hours.]

OBSERVE: courage in face of death
ILLUSTRATION: Paul—Acts 21:13
(house of Philip in Caesarea)

(The reason Paul could say, **"I'm ready to die,"** on road to **Jerusalem** is that he learned how to **live** on the road to **Damascus**.)

V. DANIEL'S ENFORCED PERSECUTION

READ: Verses 11–15

A. An **uncompromising** prophet—verses 11, 13
B. An **unalterable** law—verse 12
C. An **unhappy** king—verse 14
D. An **unchangeable** decree—verse 15

VI. DANIEL'S EXCESSIVE PUNISHMENT

READ: Verses 16, 17

A. King's **commandment**—verse 16a
B. King's **confirmation**—verse 16b
C. King's **consignment**—verse 17

OBSERVATION: Another **king** at another **time** consigned another **man** to another **tomb**, but He tore bars away on morning of the third day!

VII. DANIEL'S EFFECTED PRESERVATION

READ: Verses 18–23

A. An **unnerved** king—verse 18
B. An **unfailing** God—verse 22
C. An **unharmed** prophet—verse 23

Conclusion

God needs some more men like Daniel: backbone, courage, conviction, etc.

Appeal: Who will dare to be a Daniel?

CHAPTER TWELVE

 Lions With Lockjaw

21. *Then said Daniel unto the king, O king, live for ever.*

22. *My God hath sent his angel, and hath shut the lions' mouths, that they have not hurt me: forasmuch as before him innocency was found in me; and also before thee, O king, have I done no hurt.* —Dan. 6:21, 22.

What a man was Daniel! There's hardly another character in the Bible to whom he could be compared. Daniel's biography makes for interesting reading.

Who can compare to this fearless, faithful servant of God? Who among all the prophets had such stamina, such strong convictions, such character, such solidarity and such steadfastness? What other man in the Bible displayed such courage as this death-defying hero of the faith?

We easily detect the iron strand in this prophet as we consider the odds against him as he went up against all the evil forces in the framework of a pompous palace of a pagan potentate. Nobody stands up against such odds as Daniel did and comes out to tell the story.

"Lions With Lockjaw." Look again at verse 22: "My God hath sent his angel, and hath shut the lions' [plural] mouths." Not just one lion but a den of them. A lion's den is one thing; a den of lions is quite another. Daniel was thrown into a *den of lions.*

As we look at "Lions With Lockjaw," I remind you that some of the most crucial days recorded in Israel's history are those in which Daniel lived.

I. DANIEL'S EXALTED POSITION

Look at verses 1 and 2 of chapter 6:

1. *It pleased Darius to set over the kingdom an hundred and twenty princes, which should be over the whole kingdom;*

2. *And over these three presidents; of whom Daniel was first: that the princes might give accounts unto them, and the king should have no damage.*

As we look at Daniel's exalted position, we consider, first, the perimeters of the kingdom. This was no ordinary kingdom. It had 120 princes and three presidents, Daniel being number one.

Between 626 and 562 B.C., the Babylonians ruled the then known world. In the lifetime of Nebuchadnezzar and his successors, Evil-merodach, Neriglissar, Nabonidus and Belshazzar, his great grandson—during this course of history some exciting things took place. Babylon rose to the zenith of her power under Nebuchadnezzar; then she began a decline until in 536 B.C., the armies of the Medes and Persians, under Darius the Mede and Cyrus the Persian, conquered the kingdom of Babylon. It was not an easy task.

The invading armies of the Medes and Persians could not climb over the walls that surrounded this kingdom of Babylon because they were too high, nor penetrate them because they were too thick; so they went above the city, diverted the Euphrates River and went under the walls on dry ground. And in that night Belshazzar was slain.

Cyrus the Persian and Darius the Mede ruled somewhat simultaneously, with Cyrus ruling a bit longer. They ruled 120 provinces that stretched from India to Ethiopia, the Babylonian kingdom of Nebuchadnezzar and his successors.

In our world a Babylonian system is being formed. It is made up of political and ecclesiastical elements—that is, government, or politics, and religion. They've been bedfellows for a long time. Most politicians get really religious around election time. And many times religionists get a little political, perhaps when they ought not to. This sensual world system in which we live is the last structure of Gentile power.

Bear in mind the "Times of the Gentiles" began with Nebuchadnezzar, when he overran the city of Jerusalem in 586 B.C., destroyed the Temple, tore down the walls and took the people into captivity. That period, known as the "Times of the Gentiles," began to run its course. It still runs its course today. In our day and age and time this Babylonian system, ecclesiastical-political Babylon, made up of the religious and governmental forces of our world, is being formed.

But one day our Lord, pictured in chapter 2 as the little stone hewn out of the mountain without hands, will come rolling through Babylon and destroy the Babylonian ecclesiastical-political power. Jesus will then establish His own kingdom, and there will be no more Babylonian systems, no more political-ecclesiastical systems to rule the world. For our Lord, the Son of God, Heaven's Potentate, Commandant of all commandants, King of kings, Lord of lords, Captain of our salvation, shall rule the nations of earth with a rod of iron. And nobody will bring His kingdom down, because God says that in the days of those kings He will raise up an everlasting kingdom, and Jesus Christ will occupy the throne of His father David and rule the world from sea to shining sea.

What a wonderful day that will be!

Jesus shall reign where'er the sun
Doth his successive journeys run,
His kingdom spread from shore to shore,
Till moons shall wax and wane no more.

Behold the islands with their kings,
And Europe her finest tribute brings;
From North to South the princes meet
To pay their homage at His feet.

I'm talking about King Jesus.

Have you crowned Him your King, your Lord, your Master? It's one thing to have Him as Saviour; it's another thing to have Him as King. Many Christians who have trusted Him as Saviour have as of this moment never crowned Him King of their lives. When Jesus is King, we obey and follow Him. When He tells us what to do, we gladly do it.

Now if you're not investing in something that will outlast your life, you are not doing a very good job in your "investment corner." You had better invest it in things eternal, like the souls of men and the eternal truths of God's Word.

What a kingdom! And what a position Daniel was in—the first of three presidents ruling over 127 provinces.

We have talked about his exalted position. Now we look at his prominence. "And over these three presidents; of whom Daniel was first. . . ." Three presidents, and Daniel was number one. He came out of retirement, actually from retirement to royalty. Now follow the outline. From the death of Nebuchadnezzar in 562 B.C. until the destruction of the kingdom of Babylon in 536 B.C., Daniel was demoted. Remember, he went down into Babylon in 606 B.C. as a young man of about nineteen. He was exalted, as we've already seen in earlier chapters; now he is exalted again, but then is demoted under Evil-merodach, the son of Nebuchadnezzar. He remained in retirement until God's appointed time.

God always brings men on the scene that the times demand.

For every Pharaoh there's a Moses. For every Herod there's a John the Baptist. For every Nero there's a Paul. For every enemy God has a victor. In this generation God has and is raising up men to fight the Devil, to defy Satan, to denounce sin, and to declare the Gospel.

At the turn of this century, God raised up J. Franklin Norris. After his debut into the religious world, fundamentalism was never the same. And Fort Worth, Texas, his headquarters, was never the same. I doubt that there is a person here whose life has not, in some way, been affected and influenced by the ministry of J. Frank Norris. He has affected the whole world of Baptists. Even our friends in the Southern Baptist Convention are beginning to realize this more and more. The longer we're removed from Dr. Norris' death, the more prominent he becomes in the world of Baptists.

I'm saying this: Men come on the scene and men pass off the scene, but God's work must go on. Men who are on the scene now, who have been on the scene 25 or 30 or 40 years, will not always be on the scene. That is the reason for Norris Bible Baptist Institute. That is the reason we are training fifty young men this semester to know how to build churches and win souls. For if Jesus Christ tarries, there must be some young men to carry on. I'm praying that God, out of this congregation, will raise up some and put them in the ministry so that, when the times demand men like you, you will be ready for God.

Be ready. Be available. One of the best abilities is availability. Young men, if God comes knocking—and He just might—be available. God may ring your number tonight.

II. DANIEL'S EXCELLENT SPIRIT

3. *Then this Daniel was preferred above the presidents and princes, because an excellent spirit was in him; and the king thought to set him over the whole realm.*

Because of an excellent spirit, he is preferred by the king.

Observe three things that give evidence of the spirit of Daniel:

(1) *Self-control.* The Bible says that he who controls his own spirit is greater than a man who can conquer a city. Daniel exercises self-control because he had the right spirit.

He controlled his physical appetites. Chapter 1:8 says, when Daniel was offered the wine and meat of a pagan king, he said, "NO!" Surely that meat looked inviting; surely that wine would have tasted good; and surely both were a temptation. But God did something for Daniel so that it could be recorded that he said, "NO!"

I repeat: Daniel could handle lions when ninety because he learned to handle temptation when nineteen. If you don't say "NO" to Satan, to drugs, to alcohol, to premarital sex, to pornography and all the rest of the evils, you are headed for more heartache and trouble.

Some of you ought to go back home tonight and do away with those "R"-rated videos. You don't go to movies, but you bring movies and Hollywood, with all its filth, into your homes.

Parents, don't blame your children. I wish you could hear the pleas of some of them who have said to me, "Pastor, I wish I had listened to you five years ago or ten years ago or twenty years ago."

Young people, learn like Daniel to say NO!

Daniel was in control of his physical appetites. He crucified the flesh and could say with Paul a long time before Paul wrote it: "I am crucified with Christ: nevertheless I live; yet not I, but Christ liveth in me: and the life which I now live in the flesh I live by the faith of the Son of God, who loved me, and gave himself for me."

Daniel learned to conquer the flesh. He was a self-controlled man. He denied the ungodliness and worldly lusts about him. Remember, he was in a pagan kingdom, in a pagan palace.

Paul reminds us in Titus 2:11, 12:

"For the grace of God that bringeth salvation hath appeared to all men, Teaching us that, denying ungodliness and worldly lusts, we should live soberly, righteously, and godly, in this present world; Looking for that blessed hope, and the glorious appearing of the great God and our Saviour Jesus Christ."

I hope I'll never preach a sermon but that I bring out the fact of the second coming, for that is the next great event on God's calendar. We're not looking for a better home, a better salary, better economy—but a better place. The Saviour will bring us to where we ought to be. He went away but not to stay; He's coming back again.

(2) *Genuine holiness.* We don't hear much about holiness these days. Read what the Bible says about holiness: "Follow peace with all men, and holiness, without which no man shall see the Lord." "Be ye holy; for I am holy," saith the Lord. God demands of His people holiness; not self-righteousness. Anyone can get up and testify, "I don't do this," or "I don't do that. I don't smoke, chew or run after girls." I'm not talking about that; I'm talking about an imputed holiness that comes from God.

(3) *Unwavering faith.* We all ought to be living as Paul lived. Can we say, as Paul said and as Daniel said, "I have fought a good fight, I have finished my course, I have kept the faith"?

Just suppose you are on your deathbed. Paul was facing execution. Could you say, as Paul said, "I have fought a good fight"? Could you say, as Paul said, "I have finished my course"? Could you say, as Paul said, "I have kept the faith"?

These three evidences of the Spirit of God were also in Daniel.

III. DANIEL'S EXCEPTIONAL BEHAVIOR

4. Then the presidents and princes sought to find occasion against Daniel concerning the kingdom; but they could find none occasion nor fault; forasmuch as he was faithful, neither was there any error or fault found in him.

5. Then said these men, We shall not find any occasion against this Daniel, except we find it against him concerning the law of his God.

Could they say about you, "This man is faultless in character"? Daniel's behavior was exceptional. He was faithful in his belief. When the presidents and princes looked for fault in him concerning the kingdom, they found none.

Daniel was faultless in his behavior.

He was firm in the Book. These men said, "We shall not find any occasion against this Daniel, except we find it against him concerning the law of his God."

Psalm 119:11 reads, "Thy word have I hid in mine heart, that I might not sin against thee."

Jeremiah 15:16 tells us, "Thy words were found, and I did eat them; and thy word was unto me the joy and rejoicing of mine heart."

We read in II Timothy 2:15, "Study to shew thyself approved unto God, a workman that needeth not to be ashamed, rightly dividing the word of truth." The only way to overcome this world system is to have the Word of God in our hearts and minds.

John 1:8 declared, "This book of the law shall not depart out of thy mouth."

Psalm 1 says, 'Blessed is the man that meditates day and night.'

What kind of stuff are you reading these days? How much are you reading in the Bible?

Daniel's exceptional behavior put him in good standing with God and man.

IV. DANIEL'S EFFECTUAL PRAYER

10. Now when Daniel knew that the writing was signed, he

went into his house; and his windows being open in his chamber toward Jerusalem, he kneeled upon his knees three times a day, and prayed, and gave thanks before his God, as he did aforetime.

He didn't just put on a show. Many have a lot in the showcase, but nothing on the shelf. I know some who can get up and make a marvelous presentation, but they haven't much on the shelf. It's all showcase. It's all a put-on. It's a sham.

Not so with Daniel. No putting on. He did what he was accustomed to doing—he prayed three times a day. They saw nothing different about him. He did what he had always been doing. His behavior was consistent. He had a constant pattern of prayer, praying three times daily. No show. It was his custom.

If you knew the eyes of the world were on you, would you have to change your pattern of prayer, Bible study, soul winning, tithing, witnessing and sharing your faith? Or could you just keep on doing the same old thing and have people be impressed by it?

Remember the king's decree:

7. *All the presidents of the kingdom, the governors, and the princes, the counsellors, and the captains, have consulted together to establish a royal statute, and to make a firm decree, that whosoever shall ask a petition of any God or man for thirty days, save of thee, O king, he shall be cast into the den of lions.*

If there were a power in the United States or a power in our city of Fort Worth that said to you, "You can't pray for thirty days," how would that affect you? When was the last time you were down on your face before God? I don't mean a "Now I lay me down to sleep, I pray the Lord my soul to keep" kind of prayer, but getting alone with God and pouring out your heart to Him.

". . . that whosoever shall ask a petition of any God or man for thirty days [thirty days without prayer wouldn't bother a lot of Christians] save of thee, O king, he shall be cast [not in the lion's den; that could be empty] into the den of lions."

Look at the danger Daniel encountered and the discipline he exhibited. Let us read again verse 10:

Now when Daniel knew that the writing was signed, he went into his house; and his windows being open in his chamber toward Jerusalem, he kneeled upon his knees three times a day, and prayed, and gave thanks before his God, as he did aforetime.

He prayed as he had always prayed.

I ought to say that God doesn't keep office hours.

Central is never busy, always on the line;
You can hear from Heaven almost anytime.
'Tis a royal service built for one and all.
When you are in trouble, give this royal line a call—

morning, noon or night.

We see Daniel's courage in the face of death.

What courage the Apostle Paul exhibited, recorded in Acts 21. Paul was on his second missionary journey. He had come to Caesarea on the coast. He was in the home of Philip the evangelist. He had been warned not to go to Jerusalem because they were there lying in wait to kill him. Even a prophet came to Philip's house in Caesarea and said to Paul, 'Let me have your belt for a moment,' and Paul took it off. The Prophet Agabus took the belt and bound his own feet, then said, 'The man to whom this belt belongs will be bound in the city of Jerusalem. Paul, don't go. They will bind and imprison you.'

When they began to weep, Paul said, "What mean ye to weep and to break mine heart? for I am ready not to be bound only, but also to die at Jerusalem for the name of the Lord Jesus."

How many of you could say, "I'm ready to die for Christ"?

The problem is that most of you won't even live for Him. I rather doubt that He wants you to die for Him, but I do believe He wants you to live for Him. The reason Paul could say, on the road to Jerusalem, "I am ready also to die" was that he learned how to live on the road to Damascus when he met Jesus face to face.

V. DANIEL'S ENFORCED PERSECUTION

11. *Then these men assembled, and found Daniel praying and making supplication before his God.*

12. *Then they came near, and spake before the king concerning the king's decree; Hast thou not signed a decree, that every man that shall ask a petition of any God or man within thirty days, save of thee, O king, shall be cast into the den of lions? The king answered and said, The thing is true, according to the law of the Medes and Persians, which altereth not.*

13. *Then answered they and said before the king, That Daniel, which is of the children of the captivity of Judah, regardeth not thee, O king, nor the decree that thou hast signed, but maketh his petition three times a day.*

14. *Then the king, when he heard these words, was sore displeased with himself, and set his heart on Daniel to deliver him: and he laboured till the going down of the sun to deliver him.*

15. *Then these men assembled unto the king, and said unto the king, Know, O king, that the law of the Medes and Persians is, That no decree nor statute which the king establisheth may be changed.*

Four things in these verses I call to your attention:

(1) *An uncompromising prophet:* "Then these men assembled, and found Daniel praying and making supplication before his God." He would not compromise his practice of prayer.

(2) *An unalterable law:* "...the law of the Medes and Persians, which altereth not." The king had written this law: 'anyone who prays to any other God or to any other man except the king will be put into a den of lions.'

(3) *An unhappy king:* "Then the king, when he heard these words, was sore displeased with himself..." because of the decree that he had signed.

(4) *An unchangeable decree:* "That no decree nor statute which the king establisheth may be changed." Once written, it cannot be changed.

But an uncompromising prophet, in spite of an unhappy king, an unalterable law and an unchangeable decree, went to his chamber and prayed three times a day.

What a man was Daniel!

VI. DANIEL'S EXCESSIVE PUNISHMENT

Let us look at verses 16 and 17. First, I see the king's commandment:

16. *Then the king commanded, and they brought Daniel, and cast him into the den of lions.*

Second, I see the king's confirmation:

Now the king spake and said unto Daniel, Thy God whom thou servest continually, he will deliver thee.

Even the king recognized the power of God.

Third, I see the king's consignment:

17. *And a stone was brought, and laid upon the mouth of the den; and the king sealed it with his own signet, and with the signet of his lords; that the purpose might not be changed concerning Daniel.*

The king's signet consigned Daniel to a den of lions, which should have meant sudden and certain death.

Another king in another time consigned another Man to another cave. But on the morning of the third day He tore the bars of death loose and rose again. And now He lives! Jesus Christ is alive. All the signets of Rome and all the powers of Babylon couldn't keep Him in that grave. He arose!

He lives, and grants me daily breath;
He lives, and I shall conquer death;
He lives my mansion to prepare;
He lives to bring me safely there.

Thank God for the One who is alive!

VII. DANIEL'S EFFECTED PRESERVATION

In verse 18 we see an *unnerved king:* ". . . and his sleep went from him."

In verse 22 we see an *unfailing God:* "My God hath sent his angel, and hath shut the lions' mouths, that they have not hurt me."

In verse 23 we see an *unharmed prophet:* "So Daniel was taken up out of the den, and no manner of hurt was found upon him, because he believed in his God."

God needs more men like Daniel in our day—men of courage, conviction, character, compassion and concern.

Will you dare to be a Daniel?

For a complete list of books available from the Sword of the Lord, write to Sword of the Lord Publishers, P. O. Box 1099, Murfreesboro, Tennessee 37133.